D0016680

610-

Where Do I Begin?

Where Do I Begin?

*Stories from a
Life Lived Out Loud*

ELVIS DURAN

with Andy Barr

ATRIA BOOKS

New York London Toronto Sydney New Delhi

ATRIA
BOOKS

An Imprint of Simon & Schuster, Inc.
1230 Avenue of the Americas
New York, NY 10020

Copyright © 2019 by EeeDee, Inc.

All rights reserved, including the right to reproduce this book or portions
thereof in any form whatsoever. For information, address Atria Books
Subsidiary Rights Department, 1230 Avenue of the Americas,
New York, NY 10020.

First Atria Books hardcover edition October 2019

ATRIA BOOKS and colophon are trademarks of Simon & Schuster, Inc.

For information about special discounts for bulk purchases, please contact
Simon & Schuster Special Sales at 1-866-506-1949 or
business@simonandschuster.com.

The Simon & Schuster Speakers Bureau can bring authors to your live event.
For more information or to book an event, contact the Simon & Schuster
Speakers Bureau at 1-866-248-3049 or visit our website at
www.simonspeakers.com.

Interior design by Jill Putorti

Manufactured in the United States of America

1 3 5 7 9 10 8 6 4 2

Library of Congress Cataloging-in-Publication Data has been applied for.

ISBN 978-1-9821-0633-1
ISBN 978-1-9821-0635-5 (ebook)

Life is a big, fat book.

Alex . . . you are my favorite chapter.

I love you.

Contents

CONTENTS

Where Do
I Begin?

This Is a Nightmare

My pulse is pounding. My hands are sweaty. I think I just crapped my pants.

Look. I don't get nervous. Not even when I'm about to go live to ten million people as the host of a national radio show with my name on it.

That stuff's easy. But this? Writing a *book*? A book about *me*?

This is *agonizing*.

You wouldn't think it would be so hard to talk about myself. I do it every day on the radio. And it's not as if I'm afraid to tell you embarrassing stories about myself. I mean, this whole *book* is full of stories about getting drunk and getting high, getting fired and getting dumped, getting fat and getting thin. Want to hear about the time I pissed the bed on a romantic vacation? No problem.

One time, the guy I was dating took me to Hawaii. I'd been going nuts with work, and I was stressed out and exhausted, so he swept me away to this gorgeous house we'd rented on a hill-side overlooking the ocean. Hot, right?

So, we get to this peaceful oasis, have a piña colada or two, and then within about five seconds of putting my head on the pillow, I'm out cold. After months of pent-up exhaustion, I'm taking the greatest nap of all time.

And then, well, you know how sometimes you have a dream where you really have to go, and you make your way to the dream bathroom, and you're dream-peeing, except then you wake up in a puddle of hot pee?

And you know something? I didn't try to hide it from my guy. And I have no problem telling you about it, either (after all, it's not like I peed in *your* bed). My point: Most people would never admit they peed the bed. Me? I talk about it in a book. Not gonna hold back from ya, okay? In fact, that's not even the only story about inappropriate urination in this book. I should have called it *All the Places I Shouldn't Have Peed*.

I have no shame, and no filter, when it comes to talking to you about wetting the bed. What bothers me is having to dig deeper.

I know how to ask the kind of questions that get to the heart of who a person really is and how they got that way—I do it every day on the radio. But having to *answer* them is terrifying. Jimmy Fallon recently invited me to be a guest on *The Tonight Show*. Where HE'S the interviewer. But it didn't take long before I found myself flipping the script and starting to ask HIM questions. I'm just more comfortable on that side of the conversation.

But as much as I'd rather talk about you, this is a book about me. And if Elvis Duran were a guest on my show, I wouldn't let him get away with just telling some funny stories. I'd want to know exactly how a kid from a small town in Texas made his way to New York City—how a shy, quiet loner wound up on top in a business where all you do is talk to people. And if he said, "Oh, well, just lucky, I suppose," and then tried to change the subject, I'd say, "Bullshit."

The truth is, I *have* been lucky. *Unbelievably* lucky. But I've also had setbacks. I've made mistakes—not just the lose-your-hotel-room-deposit kind, but the people-get-hurt kind. And I've learned some tough lessons the hard way—not just about the radio business, but about myself.

Which brings me back to this book—or, rather, the blank page I'm staring at that has to turn *into* a book or else the ghosts of Simon and Schuster themselves are going to come downtown to my apartment in Tribeca and burn out my eyeballs with their cigarettes.

Turning the microphone on myself like this is a total nightmare. But I'm going to do it anyway. And here's why.

My favorite thing about what I do for a living is that, even though we play music and talk about Hollywood gossip, our show is about *real people*. Even someone like Katy Perry—someone who's way more famous than you or I will ever be and talented in ways we can only dream about—she's a real person, just like anyone else.

The thing about real people is, we all go through moments of doubt. We all have pet peeves and secret fears and aspirations we're too embarrassed to admit out loud. We all screw up. We all have dreams that haven't come true—yet. And whether I'm talking to a Grammy-winning pop star or a caller on her way to drop her kids off at school, that's the stuff I think is fascinating. The real stuff.

And I'm a real person, too. My life is fast and fun and occasionally fabulous, but the stories that have shaped it—the moments that made me who I am—could have happened to anyone. And if I tell you those stories in these pages, maybe you'll recognize something from your own life. Maybe you'll realize something new about yourself. Maybe we'll be able to connect on a whole different level. Making those connections is the best part of my job. I think it's the best part of *life* itself.

So, fine. I'll tell you everything. Even the stuff that makes me cry or cringe or want to slam my head on the coffee table.

Deep breath.

Here goes.

CHAPTER 1

Me and You and a Dog Named Boo

Do you remember the first song you ever heard on the radio?

We all have certain songs that served as the soundtrack to the moments that mattered, songs that can immediately take us right back to exactly where we were and exactly what we were thinking when everything changed.

The song that your mom always sang along to when it came on the radio. The anthem that defined your teenage years. The hit single that was playing on the car radio while you lost your virginity. You were in a car? I was in my parents' bed (they weren't there, by the way). You may even remember the lullaby your mom or dad sang to you to put you to sleep. I remember Dad's beer breath (Schlitz) when he would tuck me in when I was a little kid and also my mom's breasts. I would lazily rest my head on them and fall asleep. Still, to this day, I love laying my head on a woman's chest. With permission, naturally.

I also remember that song that made me fall in love with radio.

It was 1971. A year where my first radio song SHOULD have been by the Who or the Rolling Stones. But no. It was "Me and You and a Dog Named Boo" by Lobo.

I was seven years old, and my parents, as they often did, had left me with my grandmother for the night. She'd gone to bed, and I was curled up on the couch, playing with a cheap little radio I'd found somewhere. I had managed to tune it to KLIF, the Top 40 station transmitting from Dallas, less than an hour's drive south.

What made the moment so memorable wasn't the song but the voice that filled the silence when the last chords of "Me and You and a Dog Named Boo" faded out. I don't even remember what the DJ said. What I remember was suddenly feeling like, even in that musty old house, even in the dark of night, I wasn't alone.

Old-school AM radio stations like KLIF had a distinctive sound, a subtle electronic whirring in the background that made it seem like you were listening to a transmission from a distant planet.

Actually, that wasn't too far off from the truth. If you listen to a real radio, unlike today's FM stations, which broadcast directly to your receiver (that's why they put FM antennas on top of tall buildings), AM radio is beamed up into the atmosphere before bouncing back down to earth. You're really listening to something that has traveled almost all the way to outer space (insert your own Uranus joke here).

Not that I knew any of that at the time. To me, the hum just added to the feeling that I was experiencing something like magic.

Here, inside this tiny white plastic box, was a friend. Talking to *me*. Playing music for *me*. Passing the time with *me*. All from miles and miles away.

In the blink of an eye, I was in love. Not with the DJ, specifically. Although he had a *great* voice. I was in love with radio. I still am.

I spent a lot of time by myself. To be clear: My parents were *great*. Loving. Caring. Affectionate.

But I believe they were surprised when I showed up on the scene. Nobody ever *told* me I was an accident, but I have two older brothers, and the youngest is ten years older than I am. You do the math. In any case, looking back, Mom and Dad certainly seemed to be more ready for an empty nest than to start up with a new kid.

They were both incredibly outgoing people from big, loud families who relished being part of the world around them. Growing up, Dad had shouldered a lot of the responsibility for taking care of his brothers and sisters after his father died under circumstances nobody ever really wanted to talk about. And his work ethic made him not just a rock for his family, but a pillar of his community. He worked in several civil service jobs, dabbled in housing development, even got himself elected mayor of McKinney, our little suburban town near Dallas.

More than once, he was offered the chance to get involved in big-time politics out in Washington. But he always turned it down. He and Mom wanted to raise us in North Texas, where they'd both grown up. Besides, it was never about ambition for him. It was about service to our little community. Whatever job he happened to have at the moment—elected or not—he was always at his happiest shooting the breeze with his friends, learning about what was going on around town, trying to figure out how he could help.

Mom worked, too, at a law firm run by a family friend. But, like my father, she was most at home when she was socializing. Well-educated and drop-dead gorgeous, with a church bell of a laugh she would always deploy whenever Dad cracked a joke, she could charm anyone. They were a real power couple—not because of their jobs, but because they were so damn fun to hang out with.

And that's how I always remember them: hanging out and having fun.

When I was growing up, there were dinner parties practically every week, with new collections of strangers showing up to talk about grown-up stuff long after I had gone to bed. And even when there were no parties scheduled, *Dad* partied. Every afternoon at five sharp, out came the bourbon and ice. Except for weekends, when Mom and Dad would start the Saturday and Sunday ritual of grapefruit juice and vodka . . . in big Solo cups.

Getting buzzed was always a part of the culture around our house. But Dad was never the type to drink and get belligerent. Actually, he was at his most comedic and jovial after he had tossed back a few. It never occurred to me that one day I, too, would be utterly hilarious after getting twisted (or so I thought).

It's rough to admit that your father, whom you love more than anyone, was probably an alcoholic. And, at the time, I didn't believe that at all. He just liked to drink. A lot.

And it's not like they were neglecting me. There were a lot of hugs in that house, and there was a lot of laughter. Not a day went by when Mom and Dad didn't tell me how much they loved me. For the most part, they kept up with who my friends were and where we were hanging out.

But they were busy people, and as long as my basic needs were met, they were happy to let me fend for myself while they enjoyed the hell out of their own lives. There was food in the fridge and a phone for emergencies. They figured I could handle it from there. And so, while I don't remember ever really being *lonely* as a kid, I spent a lot of time alone.

I didn't mind. I was a quiet, introverted kid anyway. And once I discovered that human contact was right there in my radio, I always had someone to pass the time with—at least until the battery ran out.

My favorite DJ was Ron Chapman, the morning guy for KVIL, the big station in Dallas. I didn't know it back then, but Ron was a radio legend, the first to bring the "adult contemporary" format to the FM dial. People loved him for his sense of humor and his free spirit (he once jumped out of a plane and broadcast live while parachuting to the ground, and another time he broadcast live from a cage in the middle of a shark-infested pool to celebrate the release of *Jaws*). For more than three decades, Ron *was* Dallas radio. But, to me, he just felt like a close friend at a time when I didn't have a lot of those.

Oh, I tried Cub Scouts and Little League and all the other stuff your parents gently push you toward when you're a weird kid trying to fit in. And I never got bullied or anything like that. But I was always so much more comfortable living in my own head—especially when I had Ron Chapman to keep me company.

It's probably no wonder, then, that I dreamed of someday having my own radio show. I imagined being able to reach out and touch people all over the world (or at least all across the Dallas metro area).

I started practicing in my empty house during the long hours after school. I'd rush home, let myself in, make myself a snack (okay, sometimes I'd boil a whole box of spaghetti and eat it all with a mountain of butter), and head back to my room to play DJ.

I took it pretty seriously. At least I wasn't in the backyard sacrificing hamsters like the messed-up kid who lived down the street. Whatever happened to *him*?

After saving up my allowance for a few months, I sent away to J&R Music World in New York City for a "Club DJ" board. It was a cheap Numark mixer with inputs for two turntables, a cassette player, and a microphone, and I still remember exactly how it smelled when I took it out of the box (why *do* new electronics have that smell?). I connected the board to two turntables that I set up in my closet, along with a microphone and a little stand, cassette players, and a reel-to-reel tape machine so I could play back commercials I'd recorded for my imaginary sponsors. My parents bought me a build-your-own-transmitter kit from Radio-Shack that I plugged it all into. Voilà: a working radio studio, right there in my bedroom closet! As "normal" as all this seemed to me at the time, I would have been freaked out if it was MY kid living in this imaginary "radio land."

After school, I'd ride my bike over to the library to find the newest *Billboard* magazine. I'd flip straight to the Top 100 charts to see what the hot new records were, and then I'd head over to Johnny's Music Shop (right next to RadioShack in the strip mall) to spend the few dollars my dad would give me for walking-around money on the latest hits. I don't think Johnny and his wife, Linda, had many eight-year-old customers. They must have thought I was a huge pop music fan.

Truth was, I couldn't have cared less about the music itself. I was just trying to be a professional. I even turned off the aquarium in my room right before showtime so the audience wouldn't get distracted by the sound of the bubbles. Even though the "audience" consisted largely of the plastic scuba diver next to the plastic treasure chest at the bottom of the tank.

Largely—but not *entirely*. That transmitter didn't have much range, but it could reach Mrs. Rollins's house next door. She was a lovely older lady whose husband had passed away a few years earlier, and I made sure she knew what frequency to tune in to after school to hear my show.

Looking back, there was something kind of heartwarming about it: the lonely old widow and the pudgy little kid, each alone in their houses, yet connected by twelve cents' worth of cheap Chinese electronics. That is, if she was actually even listening. This was long before I was worried about ratings. Back then, I was just thrilled to be "on the air."

In between songs, I'd jabber on about the artists, read headlines from the *Dallas Morning News* or the *McKinney Courier-Gazette*, and talk about whatever was going on in our little neighborhood: the weather, who had mowed their lawn that day, stuff like that.

Once, I came home from school to find some leftover cake from last night's dinner party, so I decided to have a giveaway, just like

Ron Chapman did with concert tickets and beach vacations. Later that afternoon, an older girl from the neighborhood actually rang our doorbell to claim the prize. I had to sprint to open the door and hand over a paper plate with a plastic-wrapped slice of cake so I could get back to my "studio" before the song ended. So now I was up to TWO listeners! I was addicted. I needed more.

And then, one afternoon, I had a great idea. If this dinky little transmitter I built from a kit could reach next door on the strength of a nine-volt battery, imagine what it could do with real electric power. I could be heard across the whole neighborhood— maybe even all the way to Frisco, the next town over! So I found a toaster or a hair dryer or something lying around the house, and I took the power cord out, and I hot-wired it to my transmitter. Beaming with pride and trembling with excitement (this may have been my first memory of hard nipples), I plugged it into the outlet in my little closet studio, turned it on, prepared to blast my voice across the airwaves with more power than I had ever imagined—and that's when the transmitter exploded.

The thing about having a radio studio in a closet is that there's a lot of flammable stuff lying around. I managed to put the fire out, but that was the end of my career as an electrical engineer.

My career in radio, though, was just beginning. When I was twelve, I sat down and wrote my hero, Ron Chapman, a letter asking for any tips he might be willing to share. A few weeks later, an envelope showed up in our mailbox, addressed to me, with a Dallas return address. I *freaked out*. And when I opened it, I saw that, instead of just sending me a form letter and a bumper sticker, he had taken the time to type a real response on baby blue KVIL stationery (and given how many typos and corrections it had, he must have written it *himself* instead of delegating it to an assistant).

Talk about moments you never forget: When you're lucky enough to make a connection with one of your childhood heroes, it sticks with you forever. And even today, I can still remember what Ron wrote:

Learn all you can learn about words, and how words can paint pictures in people's minds. That's what we do in radio. It's the theater of mind.

I was floored. By his generosity, sure, but also by his advice. It made me realize that the power of radio wasn't just that you could talk to people miles away, but that you could make them *feel* things. Using nothing but your voice, you could make someone lonely feel loved. You could describe the smell of great barbecue and make a stranger's stomach rumble. You could take a kid sitting on his grandmother's couch and transport him anywhere in the world. I was ready to control the universe! Get out of my WAY! Time to change the world.

Ron's letter made me look at radio from a new perspective. There was such power in the ability to make a stranger feel something—and, right away, I knew I wanted to use that power for good. Why would you work so hard to make people feel small when you could instead make them feel happy, or hopeful? *People are lonely. I can change this. Get me to a real radio station ASAP.*

My parents, although not exactly thrilled about the whole closet-explosion thing, were totally supportive. I think they were probably excited, and maybe a little relieved, to see me developing a passion for *something*. They reached out to Ron and arranged for me to come down to Dallas to see him do his morning show at KVIL.

Dad woke me up real early. We drove down to Dallas in the wee hours of the morning and waited in the parking lot for my hero to show up for work. I was half-asleep. Who in their right mind would wake up this early every morning? At exactly a quarter to six, Ron Chapman himself emerged from the darkness clutching a briefcase, looked me over, turned to my dad, and told him to pick me up at ten sharp. He turned his key in the front door, swung it wide open.

"After you, kid."

We went up to the top floor of the building, and for the first time, I laid eyes on a *real* studio: a huge mixer with dozens of sliders and dials and buttons that lit up when you pressed them. (And the transmitter! 119,000 watts! I still don't know what that means, but it sounds HUGE. You could hear it all the way to the Oklahoma border.)

Ron dragged a stool over to the side of the room. "Sit here," he said. Then he sat down, opened his briefcase, and took out . . . a feather duster.

(Relax. It's not that kind of story.)

Apparently, it was Ron's morning routine to carefully and methodically dust every surface in the studio right before showtime. Points for cleanliness, I guess. But pretty weird. I think the feather duster was the only thing he had in that briefcase.

There wasn't a whole lot of mentoring that morning. Or any kind of conversation, really. Morning DJs can be kind of cranky—you would be, too, if you had to get up that early. But a few times, when he'd say something he thought was especially clever, Ron would take a sip of coffee and give the joke a moment to really land, and in that moment he'd look over at me to see if I was laughing.

Writing this, I realize I do the exact same thing in my own studio today. I call it the Victory Sip.

For four hours, I watched Ron play records, throw it to his news guy for the headlines, check in with Suzie Humphreys roaming the streets of Dallas in the KVIL van (they called it the "KVI-Yellow Van," because it was yellow—it was one of those stupid radio things). By the standards of today's radio, it was all pretty vanilla. Still, I was transfixed. I never saw Ron break a sweat—it was just another day at the office. But, for me, it was the best day of my life. I passed out in the car on the ride home, a huge smile on my face.

Freshman year of high school, I caught another lucky break. My friend Karis Graham and I had part-time jobs together at the local Baskin-Robbins, and she told me that her dad owned a small station in McKinney: KMMK.

I begged her to have her dad give me a job—not talking on the radio or anything, just running the mixing board during Cowboys games. Honestly, I would have done *anything* to get an actual job at a real radio studio. And, miracle of miracles: Karis came through for me. That gig scooping ice cream at Baskin-Robbins would prove to be the last job I ever had outside of broadcasting. (Well, other than the one day I spent as the DJ at the ice-skating rink at Valley View shopping center. That sucked.)

It wasn't long before I managed to work my way up and onto the air. Truth be told, it wasn't hard to do. KMMK was a tiny station out in the middle of nowhere—the studio was literally in a field, a shack with a transmitter strapped to the roof. The floors were covered in mouse droppings, which was nothing compared to the filth that was a KMMK bathroom (in addition to being cranky weirdos, radio guys tend to be pigs). We had no chance of even competing with the big stations coming from Dallas. I think I probably had a bigger audience when I was talking to Mrs. Rollins from my closet.

So there was no harm in letting an eager fourteen-year-old kid take a shift or two introducing whatever "adult contemporary" dreck we happened to be playing. The music was crap. I was pretty rough. I read the cards the station owner had written— "Coming up after the break, your farm and livestock report, presented by Blackwell Feed!"—and that was pretty much all I dared to say. When I'd listen to the tapes, I'd cringe at the Texas twang in my voice and the utter emptiness of my banter.

But it was a start. And even back then, I could see where this road might take me. KMMK was a local station, but every top of the hour we would play a network newscast. And when the news wasn't on, the satellite feed would play a live broadcast from WYNY, NBC's flagship FM station located at 30 Rockefeller Plaza in New York. And I remember how cool it was to turn down the music we were playing and hear that network feed. There I was, broadcasting live from what was basically a shanty by the side of the road in McKinney, Texas. And there in the cue speaker was Rocky Martini, broadcasting live from the center of the world in New York City.

Somehow, I had a feeling I'd find my way there someday.

It just took a while.

Putting the "'Mo" in "Alamo"

I never actually *told* my parents I was gay.

Oh, they knew. I remember finding a book in their bedroom once—some guide on What to Do When You've Got a Gay Kid. OH, BOY! This was gonna be fun.

I knew they wouldn't throw me out of the house or anything. But Mom and Dad came from a different time—remember, they were in their forties when they had me—and this just wasn't the sort of thing they *talked* about. This was going to be a horrifyingly awkward conversation. So I was kind of hoping to put it off as long as possible. Like . . . forever?

Then, one day—I must have been about thirteen—they found a note I'd written to my friend Craig where I made some reference to a guy I thought was cute. And that's when we finally had The Talk.

Mom and Dad pulled me aside. (What I wouldn't have given for another closet fire right about then.)

"We love you," Mom began, "no matter what."

"That said," Dad added, "we live in a world where you will never be accepted in business, and people might not choose to be your friend, if they know that you're gay."

I just nodded. *Gotcha.* I couldn't get out of the room fast enough. And that was the last time we ever talked about it.

The relationship I had with Mom and Dad was loving, and all positive. I still, to this day, don't regret not sharing my "gayness" with them. They loved me. They were proud of me. Why make things more complicated than that?

I guess it makes sense, though, that they might have worried about me. I was already kind of a strange kid, with few friends and a weird hobby. Now add into the mix the fact that I was a gay kid in Texas. High school could have been a *disaster*.

But, for some reason, I lucked out. It was the Bible Belt, for sure—I had one teacher senior year who was *definitely* a member of the Ku Klux Klan—but nobody ever bullied me except for one guy.

We all had that one kid, right? The one who, for no good reason, set out to make our teenage life miserable? (If you don't know what I'm talking about, odds are you *were* that one kid for someone.)

Mine was Bryce. I won't use his real name. He's probably done some growing up since then, right? (By the way, word from back home is that Bryce grew up to be an enthusiastic participant in the Corpus Christi drag scene. Funny how often people who are the most vocal in their homophobia wind up finding their own truth and coming out of the closet.)

Anyway, Bryce picked on me, or tried to. "*Fag!*" he'd scream down the hall whenever he saw me. But it wasn't scary. It was mostly just kind of sad. Even then, I could see that whatever was going on with Bryce, it wasn't about me. It was about him. And none of my other classmates ever joined in. In fact, more than a few of them came to my defense.

I remember my friend Christie marching right up to Bryce and yelling in his face, "Shut the *fuck* up!" He backed down and walked away. Thank you, Christie.

But, seriously, being gay in high school wasn't that big a deal for me. I wasn't flamboyant about it—no making out with guys in the hallways—but I didn't feel the need to lock myself in the closet. I was just . . . me. And I was comfortable with that. When people would find out, they'd often treat me as if I had been diagnosed with a serious illness. "Are you okay?" "Do you need to speak to someone?"

Huh? I wasn't dying. I was just gay! And I was fine with that. I was fine with *everything* about myself. I still am.

You'll be shocked to learn that, as I came out of my shell and started to, you know, actually participate in the world around me, I was immediately drawn to entertainment. I was in the choir, I was in musicals—you know, along with other gays. I even joined the marching band. At first, I played baritone, but then I realized that the drum major gets to run the show and wave a big stick around, so a drum major I became! You didn't even have to have talent—they just put you right up at the very front and you got to bark military-style commands at people playing flutes. Have you ever screamed "FORWARD MARCH!" at someone playing a flute?

Besides marching band, though, I didn't have much interest in school. Even though I felt I was smarter than everyone else, my grades sucked.

Besides, by the time I got done with high school, I was already doing radio. Weekends at KMMK. And a part-time job at KIKM, an AM station based out of Sherman, Texas. And this was a big deal, because unlike KMMK, KIKM was a *real* radio station with real reach.

On weekends, I'd make the thirty-mile drive up Highway 75 to do my shifts. It was kind of a spooky place. I remember the station had a ton of reverb, so when I would speak, it would always sound like I was broadcasting live from a bathroom. The show was the same stuff—playing the hits, making small talk, reading the cards they put in front of me—but, for the first time, I knew I was actually talking to more than five people. The signal from the big Dallas stations didn't make it up there, so there was a whole chunk of the state—Sherman, Denison, all of Lake Texoma!— listening to *my* show to get its Top 40 fix. I had *arrived*.

And then I got fired. The program director called my parents' house, asked to speak to me, and told me, "We're not gonna put you on the schedule this weekend."

"Okay," I said. "How come?"

There was a brief pause. "I really don't think radio is for you."

So, yeah, I'll go ahead and use *that* guy's real name: Bob McKenzie. M-C-K-E-N-Z-I-E. And no, I'm not still bitter about it. (Hey, if I spent this whole book getting revenge on everyone who's ever fired me, it'd be about eight hundred pages long.)

Even with my first firing on my record, I was ready to jump into the world of radio full-time after high school.

I had signed up for college at North Texas State University, about a half-hour drive away from home, but that was mostly an excuse to get drunk and high somewhere other than my parents' house.

I had been going to gay bars in Dallas since I was sixteen, when I'd gotten a fake ID (back then, the drinking age was eighteen, so it wasn't too much of a stretch). But it was when I left McKinney that I *really* began my long and successful career in twinkdom. Fun fact: Back then, young gay guys were called "Twinkies" and "chickens." And I spent my weekends running away from "chicken hawks."

On Sunday nights, my friends and I would hang out at the Landing, which shared a parking lot with a Mexican restaurant my parents loved to go to. The scene at the Landing, though, was nothing like our family dinners at Casa Dominguez. Sunday nights were drag night, and I never missed a chance to hang out with the drag queens, especially my favorites, Hot Chocolate and Candy Cane. Sounds like a cozy night by the Christmas tree. It was not.

On Wednesdays, we'd hit up Village Station, where they had "Dime Drink Nights." Sure, it was the shittiest liquor they could find, but a ten-cent drink is a ten-cent drink. We went hard on Wednesdays. I'd show up with a twenty in my pocket and somehow manage to leave with empty pockets—not to mention a vicious hangover-in-the-making that could only be averted by downing a plate of cinnamon waffles (another great drag name) at Lucas B&B, the gayborhood's liveliest late-night diner.

Of course, I was still living at my parents' house then, so I couldn't take home any of the guys I met at the bars. Once or twice, I woke up at a stranger's house. And if we were in a hurry, there was always that parking lot. Don't slut-shame me.

Anyway, the point is: By the time I was eighteen, I was officially out of my shell and ready to party. And while I commuted back and forth for a while, my high school friend (and gay-bar dancing partner) Melissa and I eventually went in on an apartment near campus with a rotating cast of roommates.

Melissa's one of the most lively people I've ever met: a beautiful, boisterous character who's always laughing way too loud at something totally inappropriate. We were wild in that apartment. We smoked *so much pot* in that apartment. I'd tell you more, but, honestly, all the martinis and all the bounced checks and all the one-night stands kind of blur together. I guess the best stories are the ones you only sort of remember.

I *do* remember frequently driving back to McKinney in the dead of night, half-asleep, to do mornings at KMMK. My shift started at 6 a.m., but I was always supposed to be there at five forty-five, because it was my job to flip the switches that actually turned the whole station on and booted up the transmitter.

I even made it on time, occasionally! Once I stumbled through the door at exactly six (it *might* have been 6:05, if I'm being totally honest) and heard the phone ringing off the hook. I knew who it was. C. R. Graham, the station owner, was an early riser, and he was calling to find out why the hell his station wasn't on the air. With a little bit of drunk genius, I popped a record on the turntable, dropped the needle in the middle of a song, then turned on the transmitter and picked up the phone.

"Uh, yes," I stammered, "KMMK, good morning!"

"Why aren't you on the air?!"

"Huh? We're on the air, sir. Lemme go check the transmitter. Maybe there's a problem with it."

And that was the work ethic I applied to stuff I *liked*. As for my college studies, well, let's just say I had a lot invested in finding a full-time job in radio. I spent a good deal of time putting together tapes of my (more sober) work on KMMK and sending them out to program directors all across the country. The response was underwhelming, to put it gently. Pretty much everyone who bothered to call me back told me I sucked.

The only positive response came from E. Z. McGee, the program director at KITY in San Antonio—"All-Hit KITTY," went the dumbest tagline I think I have ever heard. Cat lovers hated this radio station. With good reason.

"I believe in you," he said. "We can do something with you." E. Z. offered me a job doing nights.

"I've never even heard of that station," I told him.

"Most people haven't," he said.

But I took the job anyway. My college career wasn't going anywhere. I wasn't even really *going to college*. I was just partying *at* a college. I didn't even know where my classes were. My chances of ever getting a degree were about the same as my odds of getting back the security deposit on that apartment. So, goodbye college. Hello, San Antonio.

My friends Craig and Joe helped me pack a U-Haul with the three or four pieces of furniture I owned, and we made the three-hour drive.

The idea was that they'd stick around to help me unpack, but on the way down, we heard on the radio that there was a chance of snow. Craig and Joe panicked. Texans, you see, aren't snow people, and I guess they were worried that they might wind up stranded in San Antonio forever. So we unpacked fast and returned the U-Haul, and I dropped them off at the airport in time to catch the last flight back to Dallas just as the first flakes were falling.

And thus, that night, I found myself alone again, sitting in my big, empty apartment on my crappy old love seat.

It could have been a nice moment for self-reflection, but it lasted all of forty minutes before I decided I had to get out and see this brand-new world of mine. So I hopped in my Corolla and went for a spin—literally. It was sleeting, and I was slipping and sliding all over the highway with a big smile on my face. I thought about how, the next day, my show would be playing in all those houses I was driving by. Or it would if KITY had any listeners. Which it didn't.

But I had my first real job in a real market, not to mention my first opportunity to really live away from my parents. I was twenty years old, a college dropout, getting ready to make twelve thousand dollars a year doing nights for a station with almost no listeners.

I'm not sure I've ever been happier.

Every night at six, I'd fight the butterflies in my stomach for four hours while I did my show. I still remember the first song I played—it was "Can't Fight This Feeling" by REO Speedwagon—and, hearing my voice in the headphones, I thought, *Wow, I sound like a real DJ.*

The reason I got into radio was to paint word pictures in people's heads and make a meaningful impact on their lives. Was I doing that? No. Not really.

I was, however, having a *blast*.

During the day, I'd go out in the jankety KITY prize van. Jack Roth, the guy who owned the station, was the cheapest man alive, so our prizes consisted of whatever crap we had lying around. I think one time I had to proudly give away roach motels, courtesy of "All-Hit KITTY."

Then I'd pop by the studio to hang out with the guy whose shift was right before mine, and we'd spark up a joint while he played his records. When my own shift was done, I'd go kill an hour with a margarita nearby and wait for my friend Drex, who did the night shift on KTFM, the other Top 40 station in town, to finish up so we could hit the town together.

That was probably a no-no, hanging out with the competition, but we weren't really *competing*. KTFM was way, way ahead of us in the ratings. They had tens of thousands of listeners. We had . . . tens of listeners. Besides, the radio business back then barely felt like a business at all. Most of us were primarily in it for the good times. I was still living the college life, except I didn't have to pretend to care about classes. And San Antonio back then was one big party with its own area code.

There was one music director in town (I'm being nice and withholding his name) who would always have a line of friends and well-wishers outside his studio. They were there for the drinks that were always flowing—and for the, uh, *party favors* he always had available.

Every Tuesday (which, perhaps not coincidentally, was the day radio stations would announce which songs had made their playlist for the upcoming week), he would get a FedEx package, which was a fairly new phenomenon back then. Inside the envelope was enough coke to keep all of San Antonio going for another week. So, artists got airplay and we all got high. What a business! (By the way, to answer your question, yes, this was very illegal—look up *payola*.)

I was high on life. I was also high on drugs. And I also drank an *ocean* of tequila. Most of it happened around this divey gay bar called the Copa. I made good friends and got laid a lot. It was the perfect life for a radio DJ.

San Antonio was a city of firsts. First job. And first cell phone. It belonged to the station, and it came in a huge black canvas bag the size of a suitcase.

I was *hot shit* with that thing. I lugged it all around town, and even though you had to open it up and hoist the antenna every time you wanted to make a call, it never failed to impress the boys. We would sit outside on the patio of one of San Antonio's incredible Mexican restaurants, eating grilled goat, getting hammered on margaritas, trying to pick up guys by showing off this fancy new toy.

Until one night I made the mistake of leaving it in my car, and, of course, someone swiped it.

I owed the station eight hundred dollars, but everybody got over it pretty fast. Nothing could stop the party back then. Especially during Fiesta, the annual weeklong Mardi Gras–style extravaganza. I'd regularly wake up in the morning (okay, afternoon) to shower for work and find confetti blowing out of my underwear.

One night, I was in the studio, probably still trying to shake off the cobwebs from the previous evening's abuses, when KITY's program director, Brian White, walked in and told me they were moving me to mornings.

Morning radio. A whole new ball game. When you're doing afternoons or nights, your job is just to keep the music going. Introduce the songs. Read the commercials. Do the giveaways. But you're a *disc jockey* in the true sense of the term—everything's based on getting to the next song.

In the mornings, though, you're not the party friend. You're the sober, responsible, get-you-out-of-bed friend. You still play music, of course, but you also get to talk about the important stuff in life.

My cohost, Linda Garcia, and I were both big and loud, and we had great chemistry. But I wanted to have as many voices in the room as possible, so the conversation would feel fresh and fun. It was kind of an early ancestor of the show I do now—we had a rotating cast of voices who would pop in and out of the studio, and sometimes I'd just pull people in who were wandering by and throw them on the mic just to see what would happen.

It was so much more fun than just sitting alone at a mixing board playing records. I remember I had a character called the Weather Fairy who would "fly in," do the forecast, tell a dirty joke, and "fly out." I'd record the bits on a reel-to-reel machine and then speed it up to make my voice sound more high-pitched and effeminate. Real tacky stuff. But it was funny. Somehow, the Weather Fairy became hugely popular. That could only have happened back then. I guess you could say that in today's environment, something as tacky as the Weather Fairy definitely wouldn't *fly*.

(Sorry.)

And, no, I still wasn't changing the world, but we were having fun. Look, people in the morning are in a *bad fucking mood*. And it was up to us to be in a *great fucking mood* and win them over. I loved it. I still do.

*   *   *

At KITY in San Antonio, we had this antiquated teletype machine in the hallway. It ran 24/7, printing out endless rolls of paper with a constant stream of news headlines from the Associated Press. One night, I was wandering past the machine when the bell rang, which only happened when big news was happening. Legendary Hollywood movie star Rock Hudson had died of complications from AIDS.

Even though AIDS had been in the headlines for a few years, Rock was the first major celebrity to have his life cut short by what would become a national moral and political firestorm. And for most Americans, Rock's death was the first time they ever gave serious thought to this "gay cancer" thing.

But for me and my friends, it was already a black cloud hanging over our fun. Down at the Copa, doctors had come by to meet with the employees and encourage them to spread the word. Suddenly, everyone started thinking more about safe sex, whatever that was. Some gay men, myself included, began to back away from casual sex altogether, either out of fear or because we couldn't be bothered with condoms (I fell into both categories).

It was a really scary time. I lost a lot of friends. And even as careful as I was, I'm still relieved, and maybe even a little bit surprised, that I survived.

CHAPTER 3

Houston, I Have a Problem

AIDS was one of the two killers that always seemed to be haunting every party back then. The other was cocaine.

Coke wasn't just showing up to push records—it was pretty much *everywhere* I went. And I'd like to say it wasn't my thing, but since this isn't a job interview or an FBI background check, I'll own that I liked to play as much as anyone else did. It couldn't be all *that* dangerous, could it? After all, *everybody* was doing it. I don't think I ever once paid for the stuff (sorry, everybody I hung out with), but no matter where you went, someone had a bump to share. And we were all just having fun. Right? *Right?*

In San Antonio, I drank a lot and drugged a little. But it was always recreational. I knew when to stop.

Houston was a different story.

In 1986, I got a call from Paul Christy, the morning DJ and program director for KRBE in Houston, offering me a job doing nights at his station.

You gotta understand: If getting a full-time job in a market like San Antonio was big, this was *huge*. Houston was one of the ten biggest markets in the country, and KRBE was a *legendary* station—the first Top 40 FM station in the country to reach number one in its market. And, even better, it was *loud*. The signal bounced all over the Gulf Coast. You always knew when you were listening to KRBE. It just *sounded* big.

So even though it meant leaving behind my new family in San Antonio—and going back to doing nights—I jumped at the chance. It was a huge break. But not everyone at KRBE was thrilled to see me. My new time slot—7 to 10 p.m.—had belonged to a DJ named Casi Love. She was getting bumped to late nights to make room for me. And she was *pissed off*.

On the air, Casi had a silky smooth personality. But *off* the air, she was someone you didn't want to cross. She was a tough tomboy who didn't take crap from anyone, and she was *not* happy about getting pushed out of her time slot for this new guy. Recognizing the dangerous politics of the situation, I tried to smooth things over, telling Casi, "Don't worry—we're going to be good friends."

"We'll see," she snorted, as she grabbed her things and stormed out of the room.

Kind of a weird start! And, frankly, Houston gave me a strange, off-putting vibe from the jump. I had moved there not long after the oil industry had crashed, and a lot of the big companies in town were downsizing. Everywhere you went, you'd see boarded-up houses and closed-down businesses. Sometimes, it felt like everyone you walked by on the street had a hungry, desperate look in their eyes, like they hadn't had a good meal or a good night's sleep in far too long.

Or maybe they were just coked out. Houston was Drugs Central. The big hangout was the bar at the Four Seasons hotel, the Black Swan. You could hand the bartender a credit card, and then ten minutes later you would stroll casually into the front hallway and lift up the bowl of matchbooks at the maître d' table to find your coke neatly packaged up and ready to enjoy. Like Uber, for drugs!

That was just how Houston was back then. Coke was everywhere. Everyone was skiing, all the time. Even at work. At KRBE, you'd wander into certain people's studios or offices any time of day, and they would discreetly offer a bump, and then you'd go right back to work. Nothing unusual. Just the way it was.

And that was at the *office*. Off the clock, the party went all night long. Houston was home base for a lot of record company executives I'd gotten to know, and so there was always someone around with an expense account to pay for the night.

We used to travel to New Orleans to get crazy, and we'd stay at this old hotel called Le Richelieu, where I'd rent the big suite on the top floor. It felt like walking into the attic of the Haunted Mansion at Disney World. Creepy as hell, but an amazing place. It's still there. My crew of music industry friends would take over the bar downstairs, where Lester, the infamous bartender, would insist on making us his favorite drink: the Wedding Cake. I don't know what kind of liquor went into a Wedding Cake, but I do know it included about a half cup of powdered sugar, because I'd always end up wearing a bunch of it as a mustache. So if you ever ran into me in New Orleans in the mid-'80s, that actually *was* powdered sugar all over my face.

No matter which bar I turned up at back then, I'd always find plenty of fun people to play with. But my favorite of them all was a guy I met at the office.

His name was Terry, and he was on the air and worked in production at KRBE, recording commercials and splicing and editing tape (this was back in the pre-digital Stone Age, when making radio involved things like razor blades and Scotch tape). Terry was super sweet and had dark, Mediterranean features—and he partied! I'd never dated an Italian-American guy before. It was the beginning of my attraction to descendants of the "old country."

Lots of guys had washed in and out of my life over the past few years. Some of them quickly. A few of them not quickly enough. But, for some reason, Terry and I fit together in a more meaningful way. We worked together, which meant that I could see how hard he worked and how much dedication and talent he brought to the radio business. As we started spending more and more time together, I realized that, in addition to having a big personality, Terry was kind and generous and had a huge heart.

And, before I even knew what was happening, he was my *boyfriend*—the first serious relationship I'd ever been in.

Terry wasn't the only bright spot at work. It turned out that I had been right about Casi Love: Once we got to know each other—and she got over the insult of being moved off her time slot—she and I *did* become dear, dear friends. We loved our time together, especially our "crossover" time. I was supposed to turn the reins over to her at ten every night, but she started coming in an hour early just to hang out with me in the studio, shooting the shit.

So, I had the boyfriend, the work wife, the cool kids to drink with, and all the late-night festivities I could handle. Still, there was something *off* about the whole scene.

For one thing, as much as I loved having Casi's company during my shift, I couldn't shake the feeling that she was coming in early in part because she needed to get out of the house. And then I met her boyfriend and figured out why.

His name was Kevin, and, like a lot of people I met in Houston, he seemed to be living on the edge of a total breakdown. He had served in the military, and I don't know if something had happened to him while he was overseas, but he was prone to dark moods and flashes of anger. And when it came to his relationship with Casi, that translated into a kind of possessiveness that was really unsettling and sometimes scary. He would somehow creep into our studios, and I'd look up from the console during a song to spot him lingering in the shadows, watching Casi through the glass.

If you've ever had a friend in a really bad relationship, you know how hard it can be to know the difference between yellow flags and red ones—between *Hmm, I'm not sure this guy's quite right for you* and *Holy shit—RUN!* But, looking back, there were red flags everywhere when it came to Kevin.

One time, Casi and I were hanging out at the studio, smoking pot I'd gotten from somewhere. It was really good stuff. So Casi asked for the "roach" to take home. Sure, no problem. More where that came from.

The next night, I signed off the air, turned the controls over to Casi, and walked out into the parking lot. That's when Kevin stepped out of the darkness, and I saw that his eyes had gone ice-cold. He threatened to kill me if I ever gave her drugs again. Okay, A-plus on protecting your girlfriend from the evils of marijuana—but F-minus for being a terrifying, possessive monster.

I guess that's life when you're high all the time—when you're always on the verge of losing control, things can turn from fun to dark at the drop of a hat. You'd be out at some loud bar, screaming and laughing, and make a new friend, only to come back to the same bar the next week and discover that he had spun out and wound up in rehab. Or the hospital. Or the morgue. And after a few months of living life full throttle, I was starting to feel my own fingers slipping off the wheel.

One night, I came back from a night of partying to my friend Lisa's house, where I was staying to watch her cat while she was out of town. I'd been drinking and dancing, doing lines for hours, and all I wanted to do was go to sleep, but my body just wouldn't slow down. I felt like I'd been shot out of a cannon, and the only way I'd ever stop would be when I hit a brick wall. All night, I laid awake on Lisa's couch, my pulse pounding like a jackhammer. I kept trying not to think about the two friends who had OD'd that year and wondering if my heart would be the next to explode.

That was the longest night of my entire life. I watched the sun come up through the curtains, afraid to open my mouth because my heart *still* felt like it might just beat its way out if I let it, and I thought, *I gotta get away from this*.

It didn't help that work had started to suck.

Paul Christy, the guy who had hired me at KRBE, was a radio legend, and also a genuinely nice guy, a treat to work for. But not long after I arrived, he took a temporary "leave of absence," leaving me reporting to a management team that didn't share Paul's enthusiasm for my work. I did my show every night, but there was nothing fun about it.

I had only been in Houston for six months or so, but I was bored to tears at work and increasingly terrified that if I didn't ease up on the partying, I might wind up dead.

One night, I came home from Terry's, where I was spending most of my time, and discovered that my electricity had been shut off. Which, I guess, tends to happen when you don't bother to pay the bill. The place was a disaster. It looked like a frat house without the frat boys, like a squatter had taken up residence. There was always a cat roaming around. It wasn't even *my* cat. That apartment never felt like my home. That *city* never felt like my home.

Aside from Terry and a few close friends like Casi, Houston had nothing to offer me but trouble.

So, I did what all radio people did in those days: I sniffed around for another station . . . another unknown city. Time to move the boxes that I still hadn't gotten around to unpacking from the last move. I spread word through my network that I was looking for something new. And when I got a call from Bob Case at Z93 in Atlanta—another legendary Top 40 station—I accepted the offer before he could even finish his sentence. I didn't care that it was another night show, or that I didn't know anyone in Atlanta, or that I'd never even *been* to Atlanta. Terry was ready for a move, too, so at least I'd have company on the drive, and honestly, I just needed to get out of town.

My bosses at KRBE weren't thrilled. Or maybe they were. I couldn't tell. They pretty much ignored me. But I'd just barely been there long enough for listeners to start getting to know me, and, besides, I was breaking my contract, so every time I walked into the studio after I gave notice, I felt people glaring at me. Whatever. I was done.

The night before Terry and I were supposed to leave, I was packing up a few final boxes, listening to the radio. They'd given the seven-to-ten shift back to Casi. *Good for her*, I thought. At least she got her old job back.

But when 7 p.m. rolled around, someone else's voice came out of the speaker. That was weird. I knew Casi had a friend in town that week, but even so, it wasn't like her to miss a shift. Especially not so soon after she'd gotten her evening slot back.

I kept packing—the movers were coming first thing in the morning—but I couldn't get rid of the nagging feeling that something was wrong. Finally, Terry suggested we just drive over to Casi's house to see what was up. Maybe she'd blown off work to hang out with her friend. If so, it could be a chance for one last cocktail.

Casi lived on the first floor of her apartment building. I rang the buzzer. No answer. But when I walked around to the side of the complex, I saw her car parked right under her window, in her usual spot.

Then I saw Kevin's car parked right next to it.

Then I saw her dog, Pistol, poking his trembling nose through the curtains of her apartment window.

And, somehow . . . I just *knew*.

The manager of the apartment complex told us he couldn't enter the apartment uninvited unless there was some kind of emergency, but that nagging feeling in the back of my head had turned into full-on panic, and so I asked him to call the police. It was probably only a few minutes before the squad car showed up, but it felt like hours, the siren getting louder and louder in the back of my head.

With two Houston cops in tow, the manager pounded on Casi's door, and when there was no answer, he turned his key in her lock, taking a couple of huge steps back to let the officers in. Terry and I sat on the steps, not talking. Barely breathing.

A few minutes later, the cops emerged. "There's two bodies in there," one of them said. "A man and a woman."

It was wishful thinking, but my first thought was that maybe, just maybe, it was someone else in there. Maybe Casi had gone out to get ice or something, and whatever had happened had happened to that friend from out of town! Maybe it wasn't even her apartment, and she was hanging out next door, safe and sound, ready to laugh at me for being such a drama queen.

One of the officers shrugged. "Well," he said, "why don't you come on in and see if you can identify anyone?"

God bless Terry. He wouldn't let me go in alone. The cops led us into the apartment and back into the bedroom. There was a single lamp on in the corner, casting shadows on the ceiling and the walls, and the two dead bodies on the bed.

Casi was lying on her back, nude from the waist up, her neck covered in bruises that were already turning purple and yellow. "Casi," I said. "Casi, wake up. *Wake up, Casi.*"

"She's not gonna answer you," said the cop.

Next to her in bed was Kevin, or what was left of him. He'd shot himself in the head.

I've never wanted anything more than I wanted to turn around and run. But I couldn't. As soon as I walked out of that room, it would be real. My friend would be gone. So I stayed, I don't know for how long, just staring, hoping I'd see her take a breath, or that her eyes would pop open and she'd scream, *SURPRISE, YOU ASSHOLE! I'M ALIVE!*

So, Houston: not my favorite stop on the journey that brought me to where I am today. The city itself is great, or so people tell me all the time. And I still have a lot of fond, if fuzzy, memories of being young and reckless there.

But that place will always have a black cloud over it for me. I was there for barely half a year—and I got out not a moment too soon.

I've still never gotten over the shock of that night. And, as you can imagine, I lost my desire to take a ride on the nightly coke bus.

I guess you could say I lost *two* dear friends on my way out of Houston: Casi, and cocaine.

CHAPTER 4

The Long Road to New York City

Radio people don't move around so much anymore, but for years we were all nomads. And I was right there in the mix. Bouncing around the country—Atlanta, Philly, Austin, New Orleans. For longer than I should admit, there were only three constants in my life: tequila, Terry, and a big pile of moving boxes.

When you turn on your radio in your car, all you hear is a voice. Faceless. Nameless. Fatherless. Motherless. Armless. Who cares? You know absolutely nothing about this stranger narrating your commute, and why would you *need* to? All they're doing is giving you the weather forecast and the name of the artist singing the song. What else is there to know? Radio people aren't celebrities. We're not movie stars. We're not even Kardashians. We are totally replaceable. That's why we get replaced so often.

The thing you have to understand is, radio has *always* been a changing industry. Even back when I was starting out, back in the Wild West days when drunken weirdos owned the stations and DJs like me pretty much made it up as we went along, people were innovating, trying new things. The stuff that worked spread. The stuff that didn't? Who cares? It bounced into the atmosphere and disappeared.

It's funny. Whatever it is that is our Thing—the thing we're passionate about, the thing we couldn't imagine *not* doing every day—there's always a whole backstory we rarely stop to think about. All these people nobody has ever heard of doing things nobody but us would find interesting, but if it weren't for them, we wouldn't be living the lives we are today.

Like, do you know who Todd Storz and Gordon McLendon are? Probably not. Do you care? Doubtful. But it's my book, and radio is my passion, and if you want to know how I wound up being a Top 40 DJ, or why there even *is* such a thing as Top 40 radio, you have to let me bore you for a minute with their stories.

Okay, first: Todd Storz. He was the program director of a station in Omaha back in the 1950s, when everyone was abandoning radio for TV. But Todd realized there was one place where radio still had it over TV: cars. Americans were moving to the suburbs and spending hours driving to and from work. And cars didn't have TVs—but more and more of them were coming with built-in radios.

So Todd asked himself, *What would people want to listen to during their commutes?* The answer: recorded music. See, the old half-hour radio dramas and soap operas wouldn't work—what, were people going to sit in the parking lot at work, waiting for that episode of *The Jack Benny Program* to finish up? But popular songs? That might work. In fact, it *did* work. Todd built a ratings giant, and program directors followed his lead.

Then came Gordon. *His* big idea was making a list of which

songs were the *most* popular, and playing them and *only* them. If people were only going to listen for a little while at a time, you didn't have to worry about repeating songs. So Gordon, who owned KLIF in Dallas, got data from roadside diners (those juke-boxes on the table used to *work*) and record stores about what people were listening to, and every week, he'd put together a list in order of popularity.

The seven or so most popular songs, he'd play as often as once an hour—if you turned on KLIF and heard your very favorite song, you'd be more likely to come back. And as you went down the list, you'd get those songs less often. But the entire KLIF play-list was only forty songs long. Get it? Top *40*? Genius.

I never met either of those guys, but without them, I'd have had to find a *real* job.

Of course, Top 40 has many faces. And people are always messing with the format. More dance music! Less hip-hop! The least fun one, in my very humble opinion, is "adult contemporary"—that's when you take out anything with too much of an edge, so listeners can put it on in the background at the office and not bother anyone.

But the basic idea was always the same. Play the music people are into, and play as much of it as possible. And as for the DJ? Well, you'd read some local news, give some shout-outs to local businesses—but, for the most part, your job was just to keep the records spinning.

Which isn't to say we didn't have fun. In Philly, I got caught up in a real-life radio war. Eagle 106 was the number one Top 40 station in town, and Q102 was the underdog challenger. I came on board at Q102 in the late '80s, when they ditched their oldies format to take on Eagle 106 for Top 40 supremacy. The battle was on! And our fearless leader—our General George Patton, the guy we were all fired up to follow into battle every day—was a guy named Mark Driscoll.

I'd heard about Mark through the grapevine. People usually described him either as "a forward-thinking renegade" or "a total lunatic." Either way sounded like fun. And both turned out to be true. Mark was a *wild* guy. Bigger-than-life personality. True radio genius.

His strategy was to lean into being the underdog. We never sounded polished or slick. We were always loud and messy. In Philadelphia in those days, Italian-American club kids owned the streets and the nightclubs, and they were our target audience. Mark tilted our playlist toward upbeat, rhythmic music, and we boasted that we played not just the *most* music, but the most *fun* music, in town.

It got kind of crazy. It started with promos poking Eagle 106. And then things escalated. One day, I opened the newspaper to see an article about a kid named Tom Naylor who had put up a huge sign in front of the Eagle 106 studio that read: THE EAGLE HAS CRASHED, Q102 HAS LANDED ON YOUR ASS!

The reporter asked Tom the obvious question: *Why on earth did you do it?*

"Because," Tom explained, "Eagle 106 sucks! Q102 rules!"

Clearly, we had to hire this guy. Turned out he went to high school nearby, so we offered him a job after school as our intern/guerrilla warrior. We called him "Mr. Radio," and we sent him out to do all kinds of dumb stuff. Like taking an old van beside the highway, flipping it over, and spray-painting I FLIPPED FOR Q102 on the bottom. Or taking over an Eagle 106 billboard and writing SUCKS underneath their logo. Real mature.

I never really liked those prank wars. It felt like one of those movies where the slobs take on the snobs for control of the summer camp. But I did like the passion and the energy. Even today, whenever I feel bogged down by the daily grind, I try to channel my internal Mr. Radio to make it feel exciting and fun again. By the way, thirty years later, Tom remains a good friend who still loves, and enjoys success in, the radio biz.

Working for Mark wasn't just about juvenile pranks. There was also booze! I'd left the coke behind in Houston, but drinking on the job wasn't just tolerated, it was encouraged. That doesn't mean Mark didn't care about what was going out over our airwaves. Just the opposite. I learned a ton from him, like how to talk—well, actually, *scream*—over the intros to songs. The idea was to keep the volume of my voice at exactly the same levels as the vocals—Mark called it "swimming in the music"—and time my little intros perfectly to cut out just when the singing started, so that everything flowed together.

I felt more like a club DJ than a radio host. When I was doing mornings back in San Antonio, I could pause, turn the music down, take my time, have a *conversation* with my cohost and with the audience. But now I was doing afternoons. And there was a hard-and-fast rule for anytime after 10 a.m.: NEVER, EVER, *EVER* STOP THE MUSIC.

So, if there was ten seconds of intro at the beginning of a song, that's how much time I'd have to say something meaningful. It was a hell of a challenge, but I mastered it.

By the way, I never really liked that rule. And it's crazy to me that a lot of stations still follow it. The way I see it, if you want wall-to-wall music, you can stream it from a million different places. And that's not counting all the music that's already on your phone. The one thing radio can offer you that nothing else can is a live human connection with an actual person. A *friend*. Why give that away?

In any case, we took Q102 to the top of the ratings and it was my first job where I actually felt myself building some momentum in my career.

I even had a brush with celebrity the year Q102 sent me out to Los Angeles to cover the Oscars. Being a radio DJ didn't rate me a ticket or anything, but they had set up a whole radio row in the Sheraton Universal ballroom, and celebs would just file through for short interviews to promote whatever project they had going on, which we'd package up and air during breaks (along with the tags we'd get them to record: "Hi, I'm So-and-So, and you're listening to Q102!").

Anyway, the interviews themselves were nothing to write home about, but hey, I was in Los Angeles, rubbing shoulders with Hollywood big shots! That night, a friend and I were at the bar at the hotel—it was called Telly's, after aging (now dead) '70s TV star Telly Savalas—when a handsome guy tapped me on the shoulder and offered to buy me a drink.

Holy crap, I thought. *That's*—well, I'm not going to tell you who it was, for reasons that will become apparent in a moment. Feel free to take a guess.

So, one drink turned into another turned into an invitation

upstairs, and all of a sudden I was hooking up with a movie star. Yes, I had the most amazing boyfriend at home in Philly, but I was drunk and, well, *movie star*. I was weak. But did I mention he was a *movie star*?

I later found out that this was sort of this guy's pattern—allegedly, he frequented the Sheraton and lurked at the bar, waiting for unsuspecting out-of-towners who looked like they might make for a fun night and wowing them upstairs with his famous face.

So, you're asking, *how was it?* Meh. He was a nice guy. Kinda sad.

But hey, no complaints. At least I wound up with a couple of free drinks—and a pretty good story.

So, Philly was great. And then I got fired. I've been fired a lot, for a whole bunch of different reasons. I got fired in Atlanta because they were switching formats from Top 40 to classic rock. Later on, I got fired in Austin because I sucked at being a program director (more on my managerial shortcomings later).

Then there was the time I took a job in New Orleans and, sometime between when I got the keys to my new apartment and when the truck showed up with my new furniture, the owners called and told me they were changing formats. I could stay . . . but it was pretty clear they were hoping I wouldn't. "Store it," I told the truck driver. I barely had time to finish my first Hurricane before I was out on my ass again.

Anyway, I lasted about a year in Philly before I got the call from ownership. *Just one of those things*, they said. *It just isn't working out. We're going to go in a different direction.* Whatever. I knew how firings went.

This time, though, getting fired turned out to be one of the best things that ever happened to me—because I was now free to accept a job at Z100 in New York City.

It was like getting cut from your high school show choir and then immediately being invited to perform at the Super Bowl halftime show. Back then, in 1989, Z100 wasn't just the biggest Top 40 station in the biggest city on the planet. It was larger than *life*.

KRBE may have sounded *big*. But it had nothing on Z100. Z100 sounded *gigantic*. In fact, "Z100" was pronounced "*ZEE ONE HUNDRED*," in all caps and bold lettering with fireworks and explosions. You'd be scanning the stations, and they would all sound more or less the same, and then you'd hit 100.3 FM, and *KABOOM*. It was *so loud*. A wall of sound.

How'd they do it? Well, they borrowed some tricks from the old AM radio stations that dominated the landscape back in the Stone Age of radio. They added a ton of reverb, so that the voices and music coming over the airwaves would boom and echo through your speakers. (Whenever I'd listen to my air checks, it would sound like I was doing my show while sitting on the toilet in a big tile bathroom.)

They also used lots and lots of jingles and sweepers and other electronic sounds. They stacked 'em one after another. Lasers! Explosions! Big whooshes! At the top of the hour, our station ID would sound like this:

"SERVING THE UNIVERSE [*lasers: pew! pew!*] . . .
"FROM THE TOP [*explosion!!*] OF THE EMPIRE STATE
    BUILDING [*pew! pew!*] . . ."

Then singers would chime in with: "ZEE ONE HUNDRED NEW YORK!!" [*fireworks popping, more explosions, and—cut!*]

Z100 was known as "The Flamethrower" for a reason. Every time I heard that ID, I would hit the ground like there was a drive-by going on. It probably reads weird on the page, but we were legendary for that ID, and that sound. And as stations started to copy Z100's sound, we just got louder and blew up more shit.

After all, this was New York City! People drove around with their windows open, and you had to compete with the sounds of jackhammers and bus engines and lunatics screaming about government cameras in their dental fillings. Loud was the only way to get noticed.

In fact, Z100 was so loud, it was *illegal*. Really. I probably shouldn't tell this story. Oh, what the hell.

The good people at the Federal Communications Commission had set a legal limit for how loud you could broadcast. And most stations had special processing software so they could take their volume levels right up to that limit.

Well, the experts at Z100 had realized that the FCC didn't work weekends. And so, every Friday at 5 p.m. (or so I've heard), an engineer would go into the rack room in the back of the station where all the electronics lived and push a special button that turned the levels up way *beyond* the legal limit. On Monday morning, the first engineer in the door would turn them back down before the noise police could finish their first cup of coffee.

Hey, what's the statute of limitations on breaking the noise laws?

*　　*　　*

Z100's *programming* stood out, too. We wanted to be the station that played new music first, the station with the closest relationship with the hottest artists, the station that ran the biggest contests. We claimed ownership over every event and concert simply by saying something like: "Z100 presents: Bon Jovi." No one ever explained what the "presents" meant—we just *owned* it! If anything great happened in the world, a new royal baby or the winning of a war, Z100 would plant its flag.

Okay, so some of it was a stretch. Like the whole "broadcasting live from the top of the Empire State Building" thing. Yes, the station's transmitter was up there. But the studio itself was across the river in Secaucus, New Jersey. Which, no offense to Secaucus, doesn't quite have the same ring to it.

I have to give a shout-out to the guy who pioneered this whole balls-to-the-wall style: Scott Shannon. He took over at Z100 in 1983 and within seventy-four days took the station from last place in the ratings to number one. Scott is a genius program director, and a great DJ in his own right. He was the guy who really perfected the "morning zoo" format, where a whole roomful of loud, obnoxious clowns would yell over each other. Which we still do today.

When Scott left for Los Angeles, his protégé, Steve Kingston, took over. Steve's the guy who hired me, and I'm not just saying this *because* he's the guy who gave me my big break at Z100, but he's an extraordinary figure. Not just in my life, but in radio history.

Steve fully subscribed to that P. T. Barnum–esque theory of radio that Z100 was all about: Make a big noise, and then tell everybody about the big noise you just made. But Steve wasn't just about blunt force. He wanted every second of airtime to be the very best radio we could produce, and he challenged DJs like me to work hard to make that happen.

As soon as I showed up at Z100 in early 1990, I got a shock. No more stumbling into the studio thirty seconds before airtime. From now on, I would have to report to Z100 at least one hour before my shift started. *Imagine that!*

And, what's more, I'd have to spend that hour—get ready for this—*actually preparing for my show*. Like Mark Driscoll, Steve was an overshadowing presence at the studio. Unlike at Q102, we were all sober. I felt I had to be. I can't imagine having that firepower at my fingertips and running through my microphone while being high.

When I'd arrive, I'd have to come by Steve's office for a briefing. Every day, Z100 would have a "headline"—a contest it was running, a concert it was promoting, a new album it was premiering—and every DJ on every shift would have to wrap his or her existence around that headline.

And once Steve had filled me in on the message of the day, he'd toss the *New York Post* and *New York Daily News* across his desk and tell me to go prep some topics. I was still doing afternoons, of course, and afternoons still meant playing as much music as possible with minimal talking. So I knew—and, at first, protested—that I'd never be able to use, oh, 99 percent of the material Steve was making me put together. But that didn't matter to Steve. And, after a while, it didn't matter to me, either.

It turned out that I actually *liked* being pushed to take my job seriously for the first time in my career. Steve loved the business, and he had tremendous respect for the institution that was Z100. He always used to bellow, "This is the biggest shipper in the shipping business, man!" That probably explains why he was an insane perfectionist.

For example: At the top of every hour, you'd have to announce the station's call letters: "You're listening to WHTZ!" Well, Steve would always lurk around the station hallways like a jungle cat, and after one of those hourly announcements, I heard, and then saw, his boot slamming the door open. He walked up right behind me and said, "You're from Texas, right?"

"Yeah?"

"Yeah. Well, I know in Texas they pronounce it 'dubya,' but we're in New York City. It's 'double-U-H-T-Z.' Got it?"

"Yes, sir!"

I tried! But I still couldn't say "double-U." It kept coming out "dubya"—something Steve knew New Yorkers wouldn't tolerate. So he told me to just skip the top-of-the-hour liner . . . and any sentence where I would have to say the letter *W*.

I know this might sound like a nightmare, but Steve's passion and attention to detail really rubbed off on me. Maybe it was just that I didn't want to disappoint him, but even if all I was doing was screaming about an upcoming concert for eighteen seconds while one song transitioned into another, I worked really hard to make those eighteen seconds the very best they could be, to scream something that only Elvis Duran could scream, and that could only be screamed on New York's very own Z100.

After all, why say:

Z100—Next hour, we'll be giving away tickets to see Bon Jovi at Madison Square Garden. Caller number one hundred will get a pair of tickets, and you'll be entered into a drawing for the grand prize: front-row *tickets!*

When you could say:

Z100—Wanna sit front row at Bon Jovi? Tickets in sixty minutes! Z100!

There's a big difference, right? Same message. Fewer words. And if you're barely listening on your drive home from work, maybe you don't even notice. But I did. Z100 was the world's brightest stage, and between the station's sound and Steve Kingston's inspiration, it was never hard to produce the kind of energy that kept listeners listening.

There's an old Beatles song where they tell us, "In the end, the love you take is equal to the love you make." The idea is, you get out of relationships only what you're willing to put into them. It's true of work, too. Look, not everyone has the job they want. But there's no job that isn't worth doing right.

A lot of people I talk to are struggling to navigate their careers. Maybe that's you. Maybe you hate your job. Maybe you hate your boss. Maybe you even hate your customers. And maybe you *should* quit. But as long as you're there, it's still worth putting all of yourself into whatever you're doing.

And, by the way, that goes for us, too. What we do for a living here, it's just like a Broadway musical. We all come into work with stuff on our minds. We didn't sleep well, the traffic was a nightmare, we're dreading a dentist appointment later, we're mad at each other for whatever stupid reason. But when the orchestra starts playing and the curtain goes up, *we're on.* And we have to give it 100 percent.

I think every business is kind of like show business. Whether you're selling laptops at Best Buy or driving a city bus or teaching tenth-grade biology, when you walk in that door, you're onstage. So give them a good show. Every single time.

I didn't think that way until I got to Z100. I think of those early years at the station as my graduate education in radio, and Steve as the dean. But I wasn't totally grown up yet. Thank *God*. Because living in New York for the first time was a total blast.

Terry and I moved into a small house in Teaneck, New Jersey, just across the river, a ten-minute drive from Manhattan and an easy commute down the New Jersey Turnpike to the Z100 studio in Secaucus. And I did all the silly things people do when they fall in love with New York. I looked at the city from the entrance to the Lincoln Tunnel and wondered how many light bulbs I was seeing. I stared at the skyline and wondered how many people in those buildings were having sex right at that moment. I met New York celebrities like Victoria Gotti, daughter of famed mob boss John Gotti (she brought us food when we had her on the show—great lady). I marveled at the neon and the grime in pre-Giuliani, totally unsafe Times Square. And I discovered the magic of the outer boroughs, venturing out to go bowling on Staten Island or eat amazing Italian food in Brooklyn.

You have to remember, I'd grown up in Texas. And while mine was a relatively progressive family, it's not like I was exposed to a lot of diversity. I still remember the first time I went to Jackson Diner in Queens and had real Indian food, still the best I've ever had. And of course I remember wandering down to Alphabet

City—then the home of New York's most hard-core druggies, and now the home of some of its most expensive real estate.

It was a great time to be there, especially working afternoons. Even with the requirement that I show up an hour before my three-to-seven shift to prepare, I could sleep in. And then, of course, I'd be out the door before happy hour was even over, ready to hit the town and rage the night away before getting up at the crack of noon to do it all over again. NYC at night. The Limelight. The Roxy. One time, a drag queen on a swing kicked me square in the head. I loved every minute.

It helped that the job came with a limo driver. Al the limo driver. See, my union contract specified that if I was doing an appearance on behalf of the station, I'd be provided transportation. And, because Z100 was Z100, that transportation consisted of Al's long black stretch limousine.

We loved Al. He always looked out for us as if we were his own kids. Al would zip me through New York City traffic from one "promotional" appearance to another, and when I couldn't come up with another club that was interested in an appearance from Z100's Elvis Duran, I'd pay Al out of my own pocket to keep on driving.

I was still in my twenties, making good money, living in the middle of the world's biggest party. And Al saw it all. Having a driver in NYC is the ultimate luxury, as long as that driver doesn't blab about all the crazy bullshit that goes on in the backseat and doesn't make a big deal about the occasional mess on the leather seats. Al could write a book about all those nights. The bars. The clubs. The disco fries. Thank God he didn't. And, somehow, he delivered me home safe and sound each and every time.

*　　*　　*

I was living in my dream city, working at my dream station—and I *still* had the itch to move around. I guess I just hate unpacking boxes.

So I left after about a year. And it was a big mistake. The jobs that were out there turned out to be bad fits. And, after a couple of false starts, things started to look bleak. I remember I was interviewing for a job in Kansas City, of all places—not exactly my first choice of destinations, no offense—and in the waiting room they had a sign that said something like, ALL APPLICANTS MUST PASS A DRUG TEST. They called me in for the interview and I said, "Look, we're gonna have a problem here. I am going to fail that test."

The general manager was cool about it. "Don't worry about it," he said. "Just clean up your act, and we can wait a little while to do the drug test so you can pass." Great. Now I'd have to live in Kansas City *sober*.

But that's when Steve Kingston stepped in to save the day once again. I was sitting around, wondering whether Kansas City at least had any decent gay bars and how often I'd have to piss clean to keep my job, when Steve called me up.

"How's it going?" he asked.

"Not great," I told him.

"Sorry to hear it," he said. "You want your old job back?" *Yes, please.*

Miraculously, Steve was willing to give me another chance. But Terry was another story.

All these years, he'd followed me around the country. When

we were living in Atlanta, he'd even bought me a little white cat. We named her Kitty, and we took her from city to city. She wound up being with me for twenty years.

But as generous and selfless as Terry was, all this moving around was taking a toll on him, and on our relationship. It didn't help that it was always *my* career that came first. Terry was usually able to find work, but he kept having to quit jobs because his boyfriend felt like picking up and leaving town.

He deserved better. And when I decided to move *back* to New York—almost as suddenly as I'd decided to leave—it was time for us to have a long, sad talk. We still loved each other, but this was a bridge too far. I'd be coming back to New York alone.

Terry. The great one that got away.

By the time I got back to Z100, the radio business was changing again, and Top 40 stations like ours were struggling to keep up. This time, the culprits were a bunch of guys from Seattle with scruffy beards and guitars.

You have to remember, the whole idea of Top 40 was to just play whatever people were into. Even if it meant hopping back and forth between Phil Collins and Salt-N-Pepa. But people's tastes were changing. And getting more diverse. Phil Collins and Salt-N-Pepa? Maybe. But then throw in Vanilla Ice. And New Kids on the Block. Program directors started to worry that there were way too many different sounds getting all mixed together, like we were pouring every condiment in the fridge into the pot. Did anyone really want ketchup and soy milk in the same sauce?

Then came Pearl Jam. Their breakthrough album, *Ten*, shot

out in the summer of 1991, and it opened the floodgates for Nirvana, Soundgarden, Alice in Chains—a whole new generation of hard rock bands. I loved the sound, and the message. But program directors had a hard time imagining the audience moshing to "Smells Like Teen Spirit" and then changing gears to pump up the jams with C+C Music Factory. So all this new grunge stuff got left off a lot of playlists.

But Steve Kingston—of course it would be him—saw something other people didn't.

A big part of the reason why alternative artists like Pearl Jam had never found a home on Top 40 was that advertisers measured us in large part by how many young-to-middle-aged women were listening. These women were the key demographic when it came to buying stuff, so, as an advertiser-centered industry, we catered to *their* interests, not to those of the social outcasts listening to grunge.

Except, *wait a minute*. Who *said* it was only men who were into this music? There's no way bands like Nirvana and Stone Temple Pilots could be selling so many records if *some* of them weren't being bought by women, right? And, indeed, when we did some research, we found that women loved these bands just as much as men. Maybe even more. See? Being sexist costs you money.

Maybe you *could* play those new rock bands on a Top 40 station after all! We decided to put Steve's theory to the test. Along with our friends Matt Farber (who was programming at MTV back when they still played music videos) and Sam Milkman (yes, his real name), Steve and I snuck into Z100 at 2 a.m. I put on my headphones. Waited for the song to fade out. Dead air for three seconds.

Then I opened the mic and said, "This is Z100: *New York's New Rock*." Then out came Pearl Jam. That was a cool fucking night.

Suddenly, we saw a path forward. Under Steve's leadership, Z100 leaned into the alternative revolution, playing songs like Green Day's "When I Come Around" and Bush's "Machinehead" that you wouldn't find on other Top 40 stations. We still played our fair share of Madonna and Mariah Carey—at least for a while—but we increasingly took a pass on ballads and R&B, the stuff that had fueled Top 40 for a generation. No more New Kids on the Block. No more Janet Jackson. *Definitely* no more C+C Music Factory.

"New York's New Rock" worked, but only for a while. The competition always evolves.

Down the street on WXRK, they started playing alternative rock full-time. Up the street at 103.5, a new station, WKTU, came online playing the dance music that had disappeared from our playlist and zoomed to the top.

Grunge to the left of us, club jams to the right, and here we were: stuck in the middle. Suddenly, the future of Z100 was in doubt.

Even Steve Kingston, the man who would scream at you if you didn't have a boxful of Z100 T-shirts in the trunk of your car *at all times*, jumped ship, moving to WXRK in early 1996. We got new owners, a new program director, and even a new approach to our playlist, as we started to back off the rock and go back to pop. And it started to feel like it wouldn't be long before I had a new home. Again.

In fact, it looked like that home might be right across the street at WKTU, which by now had become the number one station in New York. They were ready to sign me away from Z100 to do their morning show, and I was ready to sign on the dotted line—we'd even gone so far as to talk money, which was a violation of my contract with Z100 (note to self: Take this part out).

The first time I met with Z100's new program director, Tom Poleman, I walked into his office ready to hand in my badge and gun. "Congratulations, and welcome to Z100," I told him. "But I have some news for you. I'm going across the street to do mornings at WKTU."

Tom smirked. "No, you're not."

Huh?

"First of all," he said, "you're under contract. Second of all, we're moving you to mornings here."

I was *furious*. "Please," I begged Tom. "Please let me go."

But he was insistent. Like it or not, my next gig in radio would be as the morning host on failing dinosaur Z100. I had no way of knowing that I would keep that job for more than twenty years.

Elvis and Elliot

One early Saturday morning, soon after I arrived at Z100, I showed up at 9 a.m. to do a weekend shift. It was quiet, and I thought I was alone—until I turned a corner and suddenly came upon Brian Wilson, not the genius musician, but the host of the weekday morning show. I'd never met him before, and he didn't seem interested in getting to know me now. In fact, he practically ran me over in his rush to get wherever it was he was going.

"Whoa!" I yelped. "You scared me!"

"Good," he snarled, and brushed past me on his way.

Morning guys. A breed unto their own. Usually in a foul mood. Maybe it's the lack of sleep. Or the pressure to bring in ratings. All my morning-show idols—Ron Chapman, Howard Stern, Scott Shannon—they all had two things in common. One: huge success. Two: You do as they say or get out of the way.

It took time for me to get that. Scott had been a hard-partying character who had a "my way or the highway," ego-driven vision, for sure. But he had also been a legend in the job, founding the *Z Morning Zoo* on Z100 and driving the station's rise to the top in the 1980s. And he left a big hole when he moved to Los Angeles. In the following years, a series of hosts tried to re-create the momentum Scott had built, but the air always slowly seeped out of the tires.

That's why I was so freaked out by Tom Poleman's offer. (Which, again, wasn't really an offer so much as a threat: *You have no choice because we will sue you if you try to leave.*)

Well, that, and also I was tired of putting up with Z100's crappy facilities in Secaucus: Our studio didn't even *face* New York City. Instead, it looked out west over the Meadowlands, which is great if you like looking at Mafia burial sites. At least at WKTU, I'd have a nice view—not to mention a head start in the ratings war and none of the baggage that came with trying to fill Scott's shoes.

But Tom didn't really give me a choice. I was under contract, and he had no intention of letting me off the hook.

At least I had one thing going for me. And his name was Elliot Segal.

Elliot and I had spent the last decade-plus crossing paths in markets across the country. He wasn't just a talented producer. He was so much fun to be around. Elliot was the loudest man on the planet, and he had absolutely no fear and no filter. He would say anything to get a laugh (or a rise), and there was nothing too insignificant for him to have a strong opinion about. He was my kind of guy.

I was thrilled when Steve Kingston brought Elliot to New York to produce Z100's morning show. I was excited to work with the guy every morning as he shouted at the top of his lungs about the news of the day, swinging the hockey stick he always carried around. And when I got the job as the new host, I was hopeful that Elliot would stick around and hold my hand.

The good news, Tom told me, was that Elliot was indeed willing to stay at Z100. The one catch, he explained, was that after years of producing, Elliot wanted to get in front of the microphone and serve as cohost, too.

I couldn't understand why Tom seemed to think this would bother me. Quite the opposite: It was a huge relief. If our audience liked hearing him yell about stuff half as much as I did, what could possibly go wrong?

And so, on April 22, 1996, *Elvis, Elliot, and the Z Morning Zoo* came on the air for the very first time.

As the "disciplined DJ" in our partnership, it was always my voice you'd hear at the top of a segment or throwing it to a song or a commercial. But the show was much more a reflection of Elliot's personality. I was doing the play-by-play, but the color came from him.

In part, that was because his production experience was invaluable in helping us plan out our show. He was the architect, and sitting in production meetings, I learned so much from the way he'd plan out the show. In reality, though, the show went wherever Elliot's mind went, and that meant it went lots of places in a hurry. He'd get halfway through one thought and switch to yelling about something else, and the whole show would just swerve all over the road. I thought it was the best thing in the world.

Experience wasn't the only thing Elliot had that I lacked. Another was *confidence*. From the moment Tom Poleman gave us the go-ahead, Elliot knew *exactly* what kind of show he wanted and how he wanted to sound, and what he wanted to say—and good luck to anyone who dared to get in his way.

You could see it in the way he swaggered around the halls of Z100, hockey stick in hand. Elliot was one of those guys who always loved to question authority—he tended to distrust anyone in a management position, and even when he didn't, he worked really hard to convince them that he did.

One time, we showed up for the show only to discover that we'd both lost our keys to our production studio. We called it the "Zoodio." It was five thirty in the morning, and no one was around to ask for help, so Elliot just decided to go ahead and kick the door in. Which he did, splintering wood everywhere.

Our general manager, John Fulham, was the nicest guy you'll ever meet, but when he got to work and saw the damage, even he couldn't help but be pissed off. Elliot just shrugged. *Hey, man, we needed to get in.* John turned to me, and I felt like a guilty little kid. But I knew what Elliot was thinking: *The show must go on!* And I had to defend my partner. (Still, John made Elliot write a check to buy the station a new door.)

That was sort of the nature of our relationship. Elliot did whatever he wanted, and I did whatever it took to keep the peace and keep him happy. Elliot would ignore the station's directive that we play a certain number of songs an hour, and I'd defend him to the bosses when he decided to lop one or two off to make room for more talk time. Elliot would fly into a rage when a cartridge malfunctioned and beat it to bits with his hockey stick before slap-shotting it down the hallway, and I'd laugh along nervously.

I even started smoking, because back then you could smoke in buildings, and Elliot chain-smoked all morning long, so I figured I might as well smoke, too.

Don't get me wrong. I was no battered housewife. I loved the guy. I loved going out to lunch after the show and hearing him crack jokes. One time he actually made one of our bosses cry, and that was probably over the line, but, at the time, I just thought, *That's so Elliot*. But most of all, I loved the energy of the show we did together—even if we had no idea if it would work. How long would this last? Was anyone even listening?

A lot of what we did on the show was just silly and fun. Right before Thanksgiving, we'd bring in a whole bunch of live turkeys. We'd do the show with them squawking and gobbling away, the studio floor lined with newspapers because turkeys love to crap everywhere. Once, we fed turkey meat *to* the turkeys. "They're fucking cannibals!" We thought that was hilarious.

But my favorite part of the show was the family we started to build. Just like back in San Antonio, where Linda Garcia and I had built a morning show that featured a whole chorus of random people chiming in, Elliot and I built a stable of voices. Some were radio professionals, like Christine Nagy and John Bell. But others were just real-life members of the production crew we thought were fun additions to the on-air mix.

One of the first hires was Danielle Monaro, a gum-smacking New York chick from the Bronx. Danielle's favorite thing in the world was gossiping about celebrities, so we decided that should be her job, too. She brought her sassy attitude and her in-depth knowledge of who was cheating on who to regular gossip segments, and eventually her role grew to include the rest of the news from Hollywood. She was tough. Didn't take shit from anyone. She grew up in a neighborhood where the girl fights involved putting lemon juice under your fingernails so it would sting when you scratched them. She also had zero on-air experience. Perfect!

Over time, Danielle would become the show's loud, fun conscience—not to mention our den mother. I didn't have a sister growing up, but I had one now. Making her laugh quickly became my favorite thing to do. It still is.

Skeery Jones was originally an intern who had absolutely no production experience until Elliot took him under his wing. Being Elliot's favorite was kind of a double-edged sword, of course, because it meant he picked on you a lot. Skeery would come in one day and forget his pen, and Elliot would make him wear a sign around his neck reading I'LL NEVER FORGET MY PEN AGAIN. And, of course, we'd talk about it on the air. Poor Skeery.

And then there was this lovable, awkward kid named Greg T who worked in the back answering phones. We realized right away that this guy was a character—like someone crossbred a nervous little Chihuahua with a New Jersey frat boy. Greg was always gung-ho about whatever task we gave him, and completely in over his head in the hustle of New York City, so we started sending him out into the streets to navigate the beastly city as our in-house prank monkey.

We've put him through so much shit over the years. But he keeps showing up every morning full of energy and game for whatever we can come up with. Another loudmouth with a massive heart.

A little later, Elliot brought in Dave Brody to write jokes and song parodies. He had done a lot of improv and had sold a few jokes to Jay Leno. He'd also managed a Starbucks to pay the bills. He came to work for us for free. Even with a wife, and kids on the way, he knew this was something he needed to be a part of. Brody was Elliot's guy. Die-hard Mets fan. Terminal crank (although secretly a big mush with a soft heart). One of the funniest people on the planet—I couldn't believe how fast his comedy brain worked, and I still can't. He stood in the corner and wrote jokes, earning his then on-air name, "the Guy in the Corner." That's still how he spends his time, by the way—except now we call him "executive producer."

If you're keeping score at home, that's a total of one person with any real idea what he was doing on the radio: Elliot. And while the show had lots of different voices, Elliot's was the one that dominated, the flavor that overpowered the rest of the soup.

I didn't mind being Elliot's straight man (ha!). I loved doing mornings. And every day at ten o'clock, I'd walk out of the studio ready to enjoy being young and carefree in the greatest city in the world.

If you have never been single in New York City, you *have* to do it. I mean, if you're married, too late. Sorry. Wish I could have gotten to you earlier. But, as much as I missed Terry in the wake of our breakup, I had to admit that I was having the time of my life.

I moved into an apartment in the heart of the Village, and even though I had to be up early for the reverse commute to Jersey, I spent my evenings roaming around and making friends. Eventually, I had enough in the bank to buy a house out in the Hamptons, where my friends and I would play on the weekends. I dated and broke up. I drank and danced. I felt like the queen of the city.

But as much fun as I was having, the show wasn't getting much traction in the ratings. And while Tom could put up with our antics, the one thing he couldn't abide was a show that wasn't getting results.

And that's how I met Dennis Clark.

Dennis was a radio consultant. I bet you didn't know that was a job. And I bet you're thinking that his appearance on the scene meant we were in big trouble. It's true. We were. Tom Poleman had given up trying to straighten us out, and corporate had dispatched Dennis to do just that. We all thought he'd be a spy for the bosses, sent in to jerk our leash and spoil our fun.

But, as it turned out, Dennis was no humorless drone. He was brilliant—*that* we could see right away. He'd gotten his start working with Los Angeles radio legend Rick Dees forever ago, and worked with shows all over the world. It was clear that Dennis was one of the smartest people in the industry. And, over the course of the next twenty years, he'd become one of my very best friends.

Dennis has a gentle way about him that, until he starts talking business, might fool you into thinking he's just a nice guy.

Make no mistake, though: He knows how to do radio better than anyone I've ever met. Some of that is nailing the little things: formatting the clock so that the show has the right pace instead of feeling rushed or draggy, making sure regular segments appear at a consistent time. Stuff like that. To this day, on the wall in my office I have a checklist of radio rules inspired by Dennis's guidance. Everything from *Keep topics tight* to *Hold listener interest* to *Be welcoming and thank callers*.

But the strategy goes beyond the nuts and bolts. Dennis taught us how to develop real characters. Who *are* we to our listeners? What lane should each of us own? What do listeners expect from each person they hear, and how do we make sure we each deliver on those expectations every day? Would you ever guess this by listening to us?

So, that's part of his genius: his unmatched understanding of radio strategy. The other part—the rarer part—is that even though he deals almost exclusively with loudmouths with huge egos, he always manages to get people on board with his guidance. Even Elliot, Mr. Always Question Authority himself, liked Dennis. And, for his part, Dennis never came off as an enforcer for management. Sometimes, Elliot and I would disagree with what the bosses wanted us to do—Dennis would always listen to what we had to say, and more than once, he took our side and pushed back on our behalf.

With Dennis on board, our show got better organized, better focused—just plain *better*. And, very slowly, we started to tick up in the ratings.

Still, if you've learned anything from my journey so far, it's that radio guys are never satisfied. This time, though, it wasn't me who pulled the plug.

*   *   *

I've heard several versions of the story. In one, Elliot went to management in the spring of 1999 and told them he wanted to move on and do his own thing. In another, he just flat-out told them, "It's either me or Elvis."

The bosses didn't want to lose his talent, so they offered him a chance to do his own show on WWDC in Washington, DC, another member of the Z100 corporate family—and the station where Howard Stern really took off.

The thing about Howard is, no matter what you think of him, he is a hero to radio people. He has a reputation, according to some, for being crass, and it's well-earned, but to us in the business he's our North Star. He took this industry that too often tended to be bland—tasteless and colorless, full of formula followers and copycats—and turned it into a place where an individual personality could shine through. A place where a host could be honest.

Howard is also the best interviewer I've ever heard. He has a way of convincing people to let their guard down and show their true selves—maybe because he's not afraid to do the same.

I remember listening to him in the car on my drive home (Howard's show was on at the same time as ours, so I had to listen to the replay). At that point I was living an hour away in rural New Jersey. I loved the long ride because I got to spend it listening to Howard. Sometimes I'd get home and then spend another hour sitting in the driveway listening to his show.

We *all* felt that way. If Pusha T is your favorite rapper's favorite rapper, Howard Stern is your favorite DJ's favorite DJ. I occasionally hear that he says nice things about me, and it always fills me with a mixture of pride and relief—because I can't imagine what I'd do if I found out he hated my guts. He's my dream guest.

But we've never been able to get him on the show, which I guess makes sense, because he works mornings, too.

I did meet him. Once. It was at a benefit for the North Shore Animal League out on Long Island. You wouldn't imagine Howard as the kind of guy to be surrounded by adorable cats, but his wife, Beth, is a big supporter of animal welfare, and when they got married, he became one, too. See? How great is this guy?

Anyway, the day of the dinner, I couldn't sit still. I was freaking out. I couldn't stop talking about it on the show that morning. *Howard's gonna be there. Howard!*

Cut to the cocktail reception. I'm in my tux, drinking way too fast, sweating bullets. And then in walks the gorgeous Beth Stern . . . and then, right behind her, the man himself. In my memory, he's about eight foot five. I hang out with celebrities all the time, but this is the only time I can ever remember being legit *starstruck*. This is the guy who made radio a Thing again. This is the guy who gave people like me permission to be honest with our audiences. This is the king of the morning! In the flesh!

Then someone notices that we're both there and says, "Let's get a picture!" Except there's a bunch of other people in the group. Including rocker Joan Jett. But I only have eyes for Howard. *Get out of here, Joan Jett—you're ruining my moment!*

Finally, everyone else breaks away and it's just me and the Sterns. Beth does most of the talking. Then Howard looks me square in the eyes and says, "So, you were nervous to meet me, huh?"

You can't lie to Howard. "I'm shitting my pants."

"Hmm," he says. "Well, is it like a *solid* shit? Or is it diarrhea?"

And so, the one conversation I've ever had with my idol wound up being mostly about fecal matter. Howard. I love him so much.

But Elliot might have loved him even more. For Elliot, it wasn't just about how great Howard was on the air. It was about how great he was at fighting the system—or standing up to his own bosses. Something to aspire to.

In any case, the idea of being able to do an edgier show at the same station where Howard got his start was no doubt appealing for Elliot. But I guess I'll always wonder whether there was more to it, whether the breakup had more to do with me than I knew at the time.

I don't know the truth about the backstory. All I know is that I got the word from Tom, we had a big goodbye party, everyone shed some tears, and all of a sudden there I was, left to stand on my own two feet.

Democracy Doesn't Work (On the Radio)

After three years of sharing the mic with Elliot, I knew I would miss his loud voice on the air. But there was something more I would miss. Unlike Elliot, I had no idea how to produce a morning radio show. And I *definitely* had no idea how to manage people.

I'd found that out back in Austin, where I'd had a job as a program director—the boss, the guy all the DJs report to. It was a disaster. Every time I'd have to coach someone or sort out a dispute or make an executive decision that affected other people's lives, I'd want to throw up.

I *still* hate managing people. Even to this day, I try to do as little of it as possible. Yes, my name is on the door and my voice is the loudest on the show, but I don't think of myself as anyone's *boss*. I don't want people asking me questions. I don't want to interview anyone for a job, or fire anyone. I don't want to break up arguments. I don't want to be a parent. And, most of all: Don't ask me for a raise. I don't write the checks. As far as your performance on the show, the only thing I can say is: Just be the best.

But once Elliot moved to DC, I was the guy everyone looked to for leadership and direction. *Shit.* For three years, we'd built a family. Now Dad was gone and I was *not* ready to be a single mother. I would wander around the building with this stunned look on my face, telling anyone who would listen, "I don't know what I'm doing." As if they couldn't tell.

At first, I tried to run the show like a democracy. Or, really, like a commune. Everyone had an equal say. Sometimes I'd even put things up for a vote.

But a radio show *can't* work like that. It needs a (hopefully benevolent) dictator. Or else things fall apart. The trains stop running on time. There's chaos in the streets.

And that's exactly what started to happen. For me, Elliot's departure was a bittersweet parting. For everyone else, it was a great opportunity, a chance to grow their voice and take on a more prominent role. Every day, people would come into the studio and subtly try to jockey for Elliot's chair, trying to be the one in front of his old microphone.

Everyone wanted to be the star of every segment, and it was a battle every morning to see who could best mimic Elliot's snarky tone and throw in the most over-the-top punch line.

And I was afraid to piss anyone off or let people down. So I became a total pushover. If you looked like you had something you wanted to say, I yielded the floor. If you came to me with an idea for a bit, I'd tell you it was great and it would be on the air the next day.

Dennis called me after the first show aired. "Well," he said, as nicely as he could, "*that* was bad."

He was right. It sucked. We'd done so much work with him to develop a consistent, coherent show. Now we were slipping back into anarchy. I was trying too hard to be nice to everyone on the team, and so I'd turned the show into something that would appeal to nobody. I was not a leader.

And I had no idea how to fix it. One day, I was pacing around my kitchen on a conference call with Dennis and Tom Poleman, and I just broke down. "Guys," I said, "I don't know what to do."

Dennis, as always, was calm and positive. "You can figure this out," he said. But then he added: "You *have* to figure this out."

Elliot was gone. He wasn't coming back. And, as hard as they might try, nobody else in the studio was going to replace him. Tom and Dennis would be as patient and helpful as they could, but I was going to have to step up and take control of my own damn show. It was going to work or "shit the bed." For the first time in my life, it was all on me. And I woke up.

The next morning, my alarm went off and I sat bolt upright in bed with the absolute certainty that things needed to change. *If I don't take control*, I thought to myself, *we're going to lose it all.* I had to make the show my own—even if it meant pissing off some friends.

So I came into work, and, just like always, the rest of the crew came pouring in full of ideas. But this time, when everyone started pitching, I raised a hand and shut them down.

"We're not doing any of that today," I said. "*Here's* what we're gonna do."

All eyebrows shot up. But I ignored the tension in the room and just laid out the plan for the show. *My* plan. For *my* show. "Oh," I finished, "and one more thing: Today, *nobody* sits at Elliot's mic."

Time to go to work!

The change was immediate, and everybody *hated* it. That was fine. The show *had* to be in my voice. And while I didn't want to be anyone's boss, I knew I had to be a leader, not a bystander. My job wasn't to be fair and give everyone the same amount of mic time. It was to push buttons. To wake people up. To know what they were passionate about and push them where I wanted them to go. If you didn't like it, tough. Get over it.

The real me tends to be shy and quiet. I'm also the kind of person who wants to make everyone around me happy at all times. I'm a host in all senses, I guess. But you can't run a morning show that way. You can't be a leader ANYWHERE that way. Our morning show, I realized, had to be *one* person's vision. We might sink or we might float, but we were on *my* boat. And I was confident it would work. I was surrounded by the most talented professionals I had ever met. *WE CAN DO THIS!*

It wasn't in my nature to take charge the way I did that day. But I felt a little better once the show started. I guess I always get a surge of confidence when you put a microphone in front of my face.

And, really, the thing that got me to step up was that I felt *responsible*. To Dennis and Tom and all the mentors who had given me so many chances over the years and to all the other people on the show who would lose their jobs and their health insurance if I fucked things up so badly we got canceled. And, of course, to my audience. I hate doing a bad show. Even today, it happens sometimes, and I walk around the rest of the day with a bad taste in my mouth.

It's really hard, deciding that you're just going to live or die on the strength of your own ideas, no matter what anyone else says. There's such a fine line between being courageous and bold and just being stubborn and dumb. And you never really know for sure which side of that line you're on.

You just have to trust your instincts and own the results. Whatever you do in life, you have to decide that you're going to SWIM. No SINKING is allowed. There's no such *thing* as sinking. If something you do fails, you're still swimming. You're learning lessons you needed to learn. When you swim to the finish line, remember that you succeeded because you took a chance on yourself. And give yourself some credit! Feel good about it! You did a hard thing and took a big risk and here you are, swimming!

Okay, so, I was officially in charge. Um . . . now what? What *was* the vision I was going to bring to the show? What *was* it that I wanted everyone else to be doing?

At this time, MTV's *The Real World* was making a social impact. It was all about real conversations. This was the time to get real, people! Real struggles. And real relationships: with your boyfriend, food, parents, money.

And, ready for this? The relationship you have with *yourself*.

A fun, fast, and positive show with carefully exposed dirty parts, wrapped up with pop culture and laughter. Could it be done? Would it work?

One early change was to start phasing out some of the stuff that, to my ear, sounded outdated and overly produced. Dave Brody is a genius when it comes to song parodies, but we started playing fewer and fewer of them on the air. I even started trying to cut back on the famous Z100 jingles. They didn't sound cool anymore. In fact, they were starting to sound like throwbacks to another era. Even now, Z100 still plays them. They make my teeth hurt.

One thing I couldn't shake: horoscopes. Ugh. I'm sorry, but I hate the horoscopes. I mean, honestly. I've been trying to get rid of these things forever. And every time I try, listeners rebel. It's like I personally came to their house and put their dog in the microwave. So they remain. Just know, while you're waiting for yours to be read, I'm in pain.

Greg T brought up another old feature—prank phone calls. I'd never been a huge fan of those, either, but it did seem like a way to bring a little bit of much-needed rudeness back into the mix. So we had Brody take the energy he used to put into song parodies and start putting it into new Phone Taps. Much to my surprise, they became one of our most popular segments.

Actually, THE most popular. And they came at a huge cost. Each call had to be planned with the listener who was pranking their friend or family member. Multiple calls had to be made to the "victim" until there was enough angst and screaming for the payoff. Then, we had to get permission from the "victim"—which sometimes required a bribe of Jingle Ball tickets. And all of this was for the *successful* Phone Taps, the ones that made it to the air.

On the flip side, there were hours and hours spent on the failures. A "victim" that just hung up the phone over and over. Or didn't get upset and was boring. Or, the worst: gave a fantastic performance, then refused to give permission for the Tap to go to air.

You can probably guess that I detest the Phone Taps. But obviously our listeners love them. So, once again, you win!

Even with the addition of Phone Taps, it was definitely a kinder, gentler show than it had been before. One big change was that we put more emphasis on empowering and showing more respect to women. I've always had a hard time seeing women become punch lines.

Today, in our studio, Danielle sits on my right, and Medha Gandhi (we just call her "Gandhi") sits on my left. Two strong, dominant, big-personality, kick-ass women by my side, helping me drive this thing. Before Gandhi, there was Bethany Watson, and before Bethany there was Carolina Bermudez, and before Carolina there was Christine Nagy. And before Danielle? Well, as far as I'm concerned, there's no such thing as "before Danielle." She's been my sister, and the beating heart of our show, from day one.

Look, I will laugh at jokes about sex. I will *tell* jokes about sex. Really gross ones, too. And, of course, people have been making women the butt of jokes forever, especially on morning radio. But it just didn't sit right with me. I didn't want to keep doing "Office Slut Wednesday," where callers (many of them women) would whisper descriptions of their coworkers' inappropriate outfits. I would never tell any other radio host how to run *their* show. But I was going to be the one who ran *mine*.

Over time, it's become a rule we always strive for: Women win on our show. It hasn't stopped us from telling jokes, or even from telling crass, disgusting jokes. We just moved the line.

Back in those early days, I had to push back against the rest of the cast, and against radio tradition. I also had to do a lot of pushing back against the bosses.

Even though I was willing to take control of the team, that didn't mean I would always take direction from Tom and Dennis.

There's a hotline that rings directly into the studio, and only one person has the number: the program director. It's for emergencies and angry "I thought I told you not to do that bit!" calls only. It rang a lot back then.

One fight we had for years was about how much music we should play. Our music director, of course, wanted our show to have lots of it. Well, I don't *play* music. I talk. So I just started playing fewer and fewer songs. And the bosses kept getting madder and madder every time a break would run long and we'd have to drop another song. I didn't care. I knew my show. And I was going to play exactly as much music as I felt like I needed to.

Another constant source of conflict was my love of playing things by ear. Dennis's big thing is *structure*. He wanted me to sit down every morning and literally make a grid. Segment 1: Talk about the new Backstreet Boys album. Segment 2: Phone Tap. Segment 3: Wacky news of the day.

That sounded boring. And I would have sucked at it even if I'd felt like trying. Which I didn't. I'm not good at structure. Ask my assistant. He keeps my schedule. Which means he spends a lot of time rescheduling meetings and events, blowing up all that organization. I like chaos. My mind thrives on throwing away the map and just driving with no plan.

I would much rather just toss topics out onto the table one after another and see what kind of fun conversations I could get people into. Or let fate tell us what we should talk about. If someone in sales showed up at the office this morning with a black eye, let's get him in here and ask about it, and then talk about the fucked-up ways *we've* received black eyes. If someone spilled water on the table, let's not edit it out! Let's laugh about it. Let's talk about other liquids we've spilled in other places. Let's make it feel real. Let's make it feel like you're just hanging out with friends, bullshitting about the world.

I loved that feeling. And the audience did, too. But the key thing is, we had to be *friends*. Nobody wants to hear total strangers talk with each other. So we couldn't let ourselves be strangers anymore.

I think one of the reasons Dennis and I have always gotten along so well is that we both fell in love with radio for the same reason. The way he tells it, radio has always been more of a friend to him than any of his actual friends, more of a family than his actual family. That always makes me think of listening to Ron Chapman on that little radio back in McKinney. At the end of the day, as Dennis puts it, we're in the friendship business.

Friends have to be three-dimensional. You have to feel like you really *know* them, and not just a caricature. So I made it a priority to help everyone develop their characters and share them with the audience.

When I say "characters," I don't mean that we're faking our radio personas. If you ran into one of us on the street, we'd be pretty much exactly like you'd expect. But I made it my job to be kind of like the conductor of an orchestra. I'd pick the music, and then I'd make sure all the right people got solos to showcase their unique talents.

One of the great things about our show is that because we've been doing it for so long, listeners have gotten to see us grow and change. You know, like *real people* do.

Danielle, for example. She used to be our fun, flirty, smart-mouthed single girl. But then I introduced her to this extremely handsome British guy named Sheldon, who I had kind of hoped was gay, and they wound up getting married, and now Danielle is our fun, flirty, smart-mouthed . . . married mother of two teenage boys. Skeery isn't the intern we all make fun of anymore, because he's been producing for twenty years and knows everything there is to know about making radio. So he's now the *producer* we all make fun of. Brody's still Brody, but he's been a cranky old man since he was a teenager.

And then there's Greg T. We used to treat him like a crash-test dummy. There was no stunt he wouldn't perform for a laugh. But at some point—it might have been after we had a truck drag him down a steep hill in a stroller, which he fell out of and fucked up his back—that started to get old.

So he started doing less slapstick frat-house stuff. No more getting shot with a fire hose. Instead, he'd do things like walk into Grand Central Terminal with massive garbage bags full of balloons, announce over a microphone that there were lottery tickets for that night's big Powerball drawing inside each one, and then release them off the balcony, causing all kinds of mayhem.

I would say that he's become more dignified over the years, but he *has* shit on the studio floor on two separate occasions. So scratch the dignity part. At least we're pretty sure we're not going to get him killed. He's also now known as a terrific father. Who ever thought that would happen back when he was breaking into listeners' backyards and swimming naked in their pools?

The more defined everyone's character became, the better our audience felt like they knew us—and the better I knew how to run the show. I could throw a topic out there and predict exactly how the discussion would go. I knew what was likely to get Danielle riled up, or what would get Skeery and Greg T at each other's throats. It made the show more fun to do, and more important, it created a better, more engaging vibe for our audience.

Oh, right. The audience. My favorite character of all.

I always think of our listeners as cohosts. Although I'll admit at first taking calls was just a crutch. If we ran out of stuff to say about a topic, or ran out of ideas, we'd open up the phone lines and see what Mary from Long Island felt like talking about.

But over time I stopped just using calls as a chance to take a break from the show and started really *listening*. That's when the show clicked into a new gear. We wanted our show to feel like a conversation among friends. Shouldn't listeners be able to *join* it?

We also figured out that there's an art to taking calls. When our producers answer the phones they make sure the callers know to get to the point right away once they're on the air.

It's not natural, if you think about it—when you start a conversation, there's usually some "hey, how ya doin'?" small talk before you get around to whatever it is you're calling about. But we're live on the air, and even five seconds of that can feel like an eternity. Just get right to that "worst first date" story you called in to share.

Once in a while, a caller will forget that. "Hi, Elvis," they'll say, "love the show!" Which is very nice to hear. But then they'll go on: "I met you last year at the Jingle Ball, and you were so nice! I still have the selfie of the two of us as my phone background. I can't believe I'm actually on the radio!"

If you listen closely when we get one of those calls, you can actually hear me grinding my teeth and choking my golden microphone. Which is not a euphemism. Although it probably should be. Please get to the point! Come to Daddy!

The best is when we get a call from someone who's in the car with a carpool buddy or a significant other—I always like asking the caller to put the other person on the phone and trying to get them to debate whatever topic we're talking about, just like I do with Danielle and Gandhi here in the studio.

And, of course, that's on purpose. Straight Nate, our senior executive producer, is constantly keeping an eye on the calls that come in—there's a big monitor in the back corner of the studio— and he'll hand me a note telling me there's someone on line eight we should put on.

Actually, we *get* a lot fewer calls than we used to. I mean, who uses the *telephone* anymore anyway? So twentieth century. But we get a ton of *texts*—yup, there's a whole other monitor tracking those—and when we get a really good one, we'll have a producer call whoever sent it in and invite them to talk about it on the air instead of just having us read it.

But one thing hasn't changed: We can't do our show without our listeners. That's what's different about radio. It's live. And, sure, lots of people listen to it later on demand, but they're hearing a show that was made in real time, with that unpredictable, anything-can-happen-at-any-moment feeling that you can only get from a truly interactive show. Even if you're listening to it months after the fact, you always know you're listening to a real conversation between real people, happening with a live energy that is absent when you prerecord.

I think all those calls from all those different people have made me a better host. It's easier to really put myself in other people's shoes now. I've never had breast cancer, but I know now that when someone is going through it, she's not just thinking about her health, but her bills, and the job she's taking time away from, and the kids she's had to put off having while she deals with her illness. I'm not from a military family, but I know now that the husbands and wives and kids of our service members are serving, too—and I always thank them.

I can't tell you how much I've learned from our audience. I feel like I've lived so many lives through them. I've gotten to know millions of people as well as they've gotten to know us. How cool is *that*? We really are in the friendship business. And the friendship goes both ways.

Our show broke a lot of rules. Actually, because we broke them, many of them aren't even rules anymore.

The rule that says you have to play so many songs an hour. Fuck that.

The rule that says you shouldn't have too many voices in the conversation. We had like half a dozen people in there at all times, and we were constantly dragging others in from outside. An intern who said something funny in yesterday's meeting. A producer who was getting married. Somebody who worked down the hall who brought in their grandmother's pound cake. The more the merrier.

The rule that says you have to abide by a strict schedule. Boring. Some hosts even sit down with their program directors after each show and listen to the air checks to see how well they stuck to the plan. Can you *imagine* me putting up with that kind of thing? I say, FLUSH THE FORMAT!

The rule that says the audience gets turned off when the hosts get into real arguments, when there's dissent and controversy. But, then again, the rule also says that the audience hates it when everyone is too nice. Whatever. We just try to be real. It seems to work.

The rule that says you have to cover up your mistakes and keep the show sounding as slick as possible. Yeah, right. Even if we had the ability to be perfectly "professional" all the time—ha!—our show wouldn't be our show without Danielle throwing up in a trash can because somebody brought in a sandwich with too much mayo, or Greg T flying off the handle because his headphones aren't working, or all of us making fun of Nate because his pants are too tight and showing off his "crab eye."

The bosses and consultants were always nagging us to clean up and fly right—until the ratings slowly started to tick up and, to their credit, they realized that maybe we were onto something.

But the biggest rule we broke, and the hardest one to rewrite, was this one: The whole show's supposed to exist to serve the host. That's horsecrap. I always felt like it should be the other way around: I was there to serve the show.

When we did some research a few years into our run, we got some good news: People really liked that our show was different. They liked that they felt like they knew all these different characters. They liked that we weren't dicks to each other, or to anyone else.

But there was one strange finding. Even though it was *my* show, I was only the fourth-most "liked" character on it. That didn't really offend me, but it troubled Tom and Dennis. How could I be New York's number one radio personality if I wasn't even the number one personality on my *own* radio show?

In my heart, I knew what the problem was. It wasn't that everyone else was hogging the airtime. Shining the spotlight on others at the table made it easier for me to hide.

It was partly that I didn't feel comfortable talking about my personal life on the air. I wish I hadn't been so afraid. After all, everybody else talked about their home life all the time. We'd have Danielle's husband or Skeery's dad call in—it was the best way to make listeners feel like they really knew us. But I wasn't that close to my own parents, and there was *no way* I was going to talk about the guys I was dating.

And I wasn't just quiet about my sexuality. I was *shy*. I know, it sounds crazy. I'm a *radio host*. I *talk for a living*. But I was always better at getting other people to open up than I was at opening up myself. Dennis would get frustrated when I'd come right up to the edge of sharing something personal and then back off before I could say anything revealing.

It took years before I could fully open up to my audience. But even in those early days, and even though I was kind of an imperfect host, we could tell we had found a formula for success. Looser. Chattier. More laughs. Less music. More friendly debates about everyday stuff. Less meanness and negativity.

We started steadily rising in the ratings. And while Tom and Dennis weren't always on board, I give them a lot of credit for working with us to develop the show into something the bosses (and sponsors) could love without losing our sense of fun.

We even got new studios, leaving behind our gross facility in Secaucus to move into a sparkling new building in Jersey City, with huge windows looking directly across the Hudson River to the Twin Towers and the greatest city in the world.

CHAPTER 7

The Day When Everything Changed

September 11, 2001, started out like every other Tuesday morning. Coffee, shower, in the car for my predawn commute to our studio in Jersey City.

I was living about an hour away from the studio then, as I'd recently had one of those NYC crisis moments where the noise, grime, and crowds had just gotten to be too much and I decided I needed out. What finally broke me was the day when I woke up and found myself having to walk through an actual chalk outline of a homicide victim on my way to work.

I was burned out. Burned out on my job. Burned out on my social life. And, more than anything else, burned out on New York City.

So I actually got in my car and drove west until I couldn't hear the Z100 signal anymore—I figured that was far enough. Dramatic, right? I turned off Interstate 78 in New Jersey into a town called Pottersville, and soon found a FOR SALE sign attached to an old farmhouse on sprawling acreage. No rats digging through dumpsters. No angry guy in the next apartment over who spends the whole night screaming at people who aren't there. No jackhammers.

Great, I thought. *Home.*

The woman working at the tiny post office eyed me skeptically. "Mighty large house," she said, "for a single man such as yourself." What year had I traveled to? Was I about to move into a Stephen King novel? I didn't care. The boxes made yet another journey.

At first, it was a refreshing change of pace. Not a lot of crime in Pottersville. But then I realized—there wasn't a lot of *anything* in Pottersville, except for horses and deer ticks. Did you know that wild turkeys sound just like screaming women?

What everybody who was in and around New York on September 11 talks about was how gorgeous the day was. Just perfect blue skies. That's my main memory of the day right up until everything changed. We were in the middle of a heated debate about online cheating. Back in those pre-Tinder days, nobody really knew what the rules were. If you're in a relationship, and you're flirting with somebody else on AOL Instant Messenger or Friendster or whatever, is that cheating? Typical stuff for morning radio.

We were all finishing up this stupid argument so we could send it to a song when I looked up and saw Tim Louie, one of our producers who screened incoming callers, cover up his phone and whirl around to look out the window.

Outside our studio was a huge living room, with a wall of

windows looking across the Hudson River at the city. I always thought of downtown Manhattan as like a theater in the round, with us and Staten Island and Brooklyn serving as the audience for the production. And through the glass, over Tim's shoulder, I could see smoke rising from one of the two twin stars that had always shared center stage.

The show had gone to break, so I pushed the button for the intercom and asked Tim what was going on. "They're telling us," he said, "that a helicopter hit the tower."

We all stood there, shocked, as the last few notes of "I'm Real"—the J. Lo and Ja Rule song that dominated the airwaves that whole summer—faded out. My mic went live.

"Z100," I said, my voice catching a little as I brought us back from break. "Eight fifty-two. Something weird is going on. The World Trade Center is on fire."

We could make out a steady stream of smoke flowing up from the top of the tower, but nobody understood quite what we were seeing. I remember thinking it looked like a volcano about to erupt. We just kept staring and stammering—and then we saw the second plane.

By then, every TV station in town had broken in with a special report, and we had one of the local channels on the monitor in the studio. When I saw the second plane hit the second tower, I instinctively looked down at the TV monitor in the studio, almost as if to ask it whether I'd really seen what I thought I just saw. But the TV had gone dark—because the local station's transmitter was on top of the second tower.

That's when I think it hit everyone—at least, that's when it hit me—that something unlike anything else we'd ever seen was happening. And we all kind of snapped into action. I became Mr. Organization, assigning people to monitor the news or make phone calls. And then it dawned on me that while Z100 didn't have any transmitters on those towers, some of our other stations did. Were any of our engineers working today? Was everybody safe? (I later found out that Josh Hadden, our chief engineer, was indeed supposed to be at the World Trade Center that day, but, thank God, he'd set his alarm for p.m. instead of a.m. and overslept.)

What else, what else? *Oh, right—we're on live radio*. But what could anyone possibly want to hear from us at a moment like that? This wasn't a newsroom. We were in no position to cover a breaking story, much less help people deal with this emergency. We certainly couldn't go back to playing music and arguing about cheating boyfriends. I was, uncharacteristically, at a loss for words. So we just found a local TV station that was still on the air, reporting on the breaking news, and turned up the audio, figuring that listeners in their cars who weren't near a TV would appreciate it.

As we approached the end of showtime, we started to hear about other attacks. The Pentagon was on fire. The White House was evacuated. There were rumors of more hijacked planes, car bombs on the National Mall, threats to other buildings in New York and elsewhere. Staffers were starting to grab their stuff and rush out the door to get home. We had no idea who was about to be hit next. Or why.

Dennis Clark, who had been staying with me while working at the station, came in with his bags packed ready to go to his next stop in Boston. I remember turning to him and saying, "There is no way you are flying to Boston right now."

"Well," he said, "then I need to get back to LA." He still didn't understand the scale of what had happened. None of us did.

"Dude," I told him, "you're not flying *anywhere*."

He laughed. "I'll be safe in LA. What are they gonna hit—the HOLLYWOOD sign?" And he raced downstairs to his rental car.

A few minutes later, as we were going off the air, we saw another huge plume of smoke as the first tower began to give way. I'll never forget watching Danielle fall to the ground as the tower did, and while our studio was soundproofed against outside noise, I'll never forget hearing her sobs from the other side of the glass. My sweet sister, Danielle. She didn't deserve to have to witness this. There's a tear in my eye as I'm writing about her.

As I left the studio, I called Dennis on his cell. By then, the FAA had shut down all air traffic in the entire country, and anyway he hadn't gotten far. The streets around our building in Jersey City had been more or less shut down, and he hadn't even been able to reach his car. I managed to get out of the studio garage and find him, and we made our way through the pandemonium, with nowhere else to go but back to my farmhouse in Pottersville, where Dennis realized he was stuck for the immediate future.

As we drove west, away from the city, we saw people on the street pointing in the other direction. Dennis swiveled in the passenger seat. "Holy shit," he said. "The other tower's falling."

I didn't even have to turn around to see it: it was perfectly framed in my side mirror, the words OBJECTS IN MIRROR ARE CLOSER THAN THEY APPEAR etched underneath the collapsing skyscraper.

* * *

We spent the day glued to the TV like everyone else. I think I left once to get gas and cash, just in case . . . well, I didn't know in case of *what*, just that it felt like a good idea. Dennis is famous for his ability to take a nap anywhere, anytime (a useful trait when you spend so much of your life on planes), and at some point he decided it was time to pass out for a bit, so I broke away from the news and wandered over to the back of the house.

It was a beautiful afternoon in Pottersville, just like it had been a beautiful morning in Manhattan. I was staring blankly at the empty space where a tree had recently been uprooted when all of a sudden, out of nowhere, a bird smacked into the window right in front of my face, just like I'd watched that plane smack into the World Trade Center a few hours earlier. *Splat,* into the window, and *thud,* onto the frame of the deck I was building.

I ran outside. The little bird was still moving, but barely. I picked it up, felt it go still in my hands. And that's the moment when I finally just lost it. For the first time it all felt real. I remember standing in the backyard, cradling the lifeless bird to my chest, crying like a baby, trying not to wake up Dennis. And even from a day filled with so many horrific images, that's one I know I'll never, ever be able to shake.

The rest of that day was a blur. Dennis and I watched TV into the night. For some reason, it helped to have TV news anchor Dan Rather walking us through it all. His soft Texas drawl, maybe. Or maybe it's just that he's one of the few people we felt like we could trust when everything was falling apart. Either way, we kept it on

CBS for hours. I didn't really sleep much. But eventually Tuesday turned into Wednesday, and it was time to go to work.

I had no idea what to expect when we set out from Pottersville in the dark that morning. With commercial airspace still shut down, I had a suspicion that Dennis was going to be crashing with me for a while, but I didn't know whether I could even get to the studio in my car. All night, I'd been telling staffers that if they could make it in, they should. But I didn't know what the hell kind of show we'd be able to do.

By the time we got on the New Jersey Turnpike, I could make out the Statue of Liberty, still standing. But where the towers had once dominated the skyline, there was just thick gray nothingness. The clouds of smoke were still massive. By the time I took the exit to Jersey City, there were guys with machine guns everywhere demanding to know who I was and where I was going. I had to show my ID half a dozen times between the highway and the front desk at the Z100 building.

There were a few staffers sitting outside the studio when I finally made it up there. "What are we going to do?" they asked. They could have been talking about the show, or asking in a more profound sense. Either way, my answer was the same: "I don't know."

Z100 was playing live audio from CNN. The studio itself was empty, the lights turned off. But as I walked in, I realized it wasn't dark. The board was aglow with dozens of colored lights—not just the digital meters showing the volume of the simulcast, but the lights corresponding to the phone lines into the studio, every single one of them representing a caller, impatiently waiting.

Without thinking, I grabbed my headphones, pushed one of

the buttons, and said, for the first of what would be hundreds of times that day, "Hello, Z100—you're on the air."

Hi . . . My dad never came home last night. He worked in Tower Two on the ninety-fourth floor. His name is Tom. If anyone hears from him, will you let him know we're waiting for him at home? All right. Thank you. Next call.

Elvis! Are you guys okay? We're fine, thanks for asking.

My car is stuck at Ground Zero. I'm on the Jersey Turnpike. I'm walking south. I need to get to Camden. If anyone sees me, will you pick me up and take me home? Okay. Thank you. Next call.

Can you play "God Bless the USA?" Sure. Sounds like a good idea.

As I kept taking calls, one after another, I remember seeing other members of the show gathering outside the studio window, looking in as if to ask what I was doing. I'm not sure I could have answered.

Eventually, nearly everyone filtered in, having survived the security gauntlet. People kept coming in, popping on headphones, sharing their own experiences. Downstairs, by the ferry docks commuters used to get to the World Trade Center, emergency workers had set up staging areas. At some point, we received our first call from Ground Zero. They needed food, so we put the call out on the air, and within minutes, delis started showing up with sandwiches.

We stayed on the air all morning and into the late afternoon taking calls. Some passionate listeners had requests—a woman who had been glued to the news all day just wanted to hear a patriotic song, or recovery workers were requesting baby booties to put on their dogs' paws while they helped search through the wreckage, or an emotional husband was hoping that someone out there had heard from his wife, who was still missing. Some just wanted to talk, or cry.

And in the days that followed, we just kept going. No commercials, very little music (aside from the occasional playing of a song like Enrique Iglesias's "Hero"), just real people talking to each other about this unthinkable thing that had happened to us all.

There were plenty of tears, but also moments of inspiration—like the day (I think it was Thursday) when we saw, amidst the haze that had enveloped the whole city, new smoke rising up from down at the ferry docks. We went over to see what was happening and spotted a catering truck from Outback Steakhouse grilling steaks for the cops, firefighters, and paramedics.

And then one day a caller said something funny, and we laughed, and it was the strangest sound—because it had been days since we'd heard actual laughter. Immediately, we all looked at each other nervously: *Was it okay to laugh yet?* It was, and I think it gave our audience license to laugh again, too.

It took Dennis days to get out of New Jersey, but in all that time, he never once gave us any direction from on high. He constantly reminded us to put ourselves in the minds and hearts of the listeners. Say and do what they needed most at that moment. We started to feel not like radio professionals, but like human beings, connecting with other human beings at a moment of tragedy and fear and confusion. We had no road map. We had no strategy. We just trusted our guts and our audience and did what we thought we should do.

Even when we got back to making prank phone calls and gossiping about celebrities and making fun of each other, we found ourselves thinking a lot more about what all that dumb stuff really *meant* to our listeners.

People *need* silly sometimes. And even more than that, they need to feel *connected*. Like they're part of something bigger than themselves. When times are good, we all want someone to celebrate with us. And when times are hard—incredibly hard—it's all the more important to feel like we're not in it alone.

Few of us, God willing, will ever experience a nightmare like 9/11 again. But everyone experiences moments of tragedy and fear and confusion in their own lives. They have a job they can't stand and a boss who treats them unfairly. They have a spouse who's grown distant or a kid who's in trouble. They're dreading coming out to their family at Thanksgiving or waiting for a call from their doctor about some tests or worrying about paying off their credit cards. Or maybe they're just stuck in traffic.

No matter what it is, they're counting on us to be there for them. This isn't just a job. It's a privilege.

CHAPTER 8

The Elvis Duran Guide to (One Percent of) New York City

It's so easy to just wander through life without ever thinking about why what you do matters. You can get up and brush your teeth and go to work and sit through meetings and come home and eat dinner and watch TV and go to bed and never once stop to think about the impact you have on the people around you.

That's especially true in a big city like New York. Just going about your business, you probably see a thousand different people a day. Well, you *look at* them, anyway. For a split second. But you don't really *see* them. They become a blur of . . . objects. Large, sometimes smelly, moving objects you have to wait in line behind to buy laundry detergent.

But remember: You and I have a place here. We have a purpose. And so does that asshole who's taking forever to buy *his* laundry detergent and it's driving you nuts. Everyone's on a journey, and our journeys are interconnected. Everything we do resonates outward. We matter, constantly, to the people in our lives and to people we'll never meet.

After 9/11, I started thinking more about the way our show could reflect that interconnectedness. It became a new purpose for me, a new reason not to take the privilege of doing what I do for granted.

I also started thinking more about how being a New Yorker means being part of something bigger than yourself.

Us New Yorkers have a complicated relationship with the place we call home. There's this joke we tell each other: "I love New York—can't wait till they finish it!" There's always construction happening everywhere. Scaffolding that you have to walk around. Jackhammers you have to shout over. Smoke plumes rising out of manhole covers for no apparent reason. You can't live here unless you love being at the center of the action, but at the center of the action, it's usually loud and crowded and it smells like pee and pot.

Yes, New York is a pain in the ass because there are so many of us walking around, bumping into each other, stealing each other's taxis. But it's also a gift. Because none of those people are faceless. Those thousand people you walk past every day? Every single one of them is on a journey. Every one of them simply wants to be loved and needed.

I think a lot of New Yorkers who lived through 9/11 wound up feeling a different, closer connection in the years that followed that tragic day. We all started looking each other in the eye a little more.

And even though I still got annoyed by the noise and the smells from time to time, I was excited when, a few years later, corporate decided to move all its New York radio stations into *actual New*

York. It felt *right* for a station, and a show, that had such a strong relationship with the people of New York to be *located* in New York.

Not only do I get to work in Manhattan, I now get to go to work in my single favorite building in the whole city—maybe even the whole world.

During my brief time in college, I took an architecture class. I loved it so much, I actually showed up for it, sometimes. One of the assignments was to write a report on the history of a building, and I picked the AT&T Building at 32 Avenue of the Americas.

It's a gorgeous, twenty-seven-story Art Deco masterpiece. But the reason I picked it was that it was the site of the very first transatlantic cable. There's a mosaic in the lobby, a map of the world made up of little tiles, and, at the bottom, it reads: TELE-PHONE WIRES AND RADIO UNITE TO MAKE NEIGHBORS OF NATIONS. Pretty cool. Yes, I am a radio geek.

Now I get to walk by that mosaic every single morning, because I work on the third floor. Small world, right?

But wait—there's more! In addition to working in the world's greatest building, I also have the world's easiest commute.

I know I shouldn't brag about this. A lot of the people who start their day listening to my show are stuck in traffic. Traffic drives me fucking insane. I can't do it.

And the good news is . . . I don't have to anymore! Because I went ahead and bought a new place just around the corner from the studio. Some days, I just walk to work. And on those days, I feel like there's no other place I'd rather be than New York City.

The neighborhood used to be called Tribeca, which is an obnoxious abbreviation for "the triangle below Canal Street." But a few years ago, someone came up with the idea that, because it's close to Chinatown, my part of the neighborhood should be called Chibeca instead. Us New Yorkers need to believe we live in our own little towns. That's what sets us apart from each other. Tribeca is wealthy families. Hell's Kitchen and Chelsea are yuppies and the gays. The East Village is for the rich who like to believe they're starving artists. And above Twenty-Third Street? Well, who cares about anything above Twenty-Third Street. It might as well be Canada, as far as I'm concerned.

No matter what you call it, there's no better time to be out and about than five forty-five in the morning, when it's quiet and calm. Manhattan's just starting to wake up, and the first few cars are trickling in from the Holland Tunnel. The whole city feels like it belongs to just the few of us who are out on the streets. There are always a few little old ladies walking their dogs, but mostly it's service workers. Bakery truck drivers delivering bread. Garbage men picking up trash.

A lot of these guys know me by now. Sometimes they'll start honking and yelling, "Hey, Elvis!" Because, you know, it's not like anyone's trying to sleep. That's my city!

Want to know the secret to living in New York? It's simple. Don't try to live in *all* of New York.

The first time you come here, you can't stop marveling at *how much* is happening, and *how many* places there are to explore. And the people! There are so fucking many people. And they're all different, and they're all fascinating, and they're always running in a million different directions, doing a million different things. So you start imagining how cool it must be to live here, and to be the master of such a huge domain, and to have all these exciting things to do, and to know all these people!

But that's not what living in New York is really like. Yeah, you're going to spend a lot of time out in the world, because your apartment is going to be tiny (even though it's crazy expensive). And, yeah, there are always interesting people to meet, people who are on their own New York adventure. But you can't see everything. You can't meet everyone.

Ninety-nine percent of your life in New York is going to happen in one percent of the city. And once you find the one percent that feels like home, the rest of the city might as well not exist. *You want me to ride in a cab for seven whole minutes to meet you for dinner? Uh, too far. Out of my zone.*

There are sixty thousand restaurants in New York, but I pretty much only go to two.

There's the Odeon. A real landmark. Oddly, I first experienced Odeon while visiting NYC the year it opened back in 1980, before Tribeca had a name. No name, because nobody went there. It was all gas stations and warehouses. Odeon is a slice of retro New York, all chrome and neon, with a great bar where I've spent a lot of late nights (and some infamous bathrooms where I've seen a lot of famous people "partying"). Back in the day it was a late-night hangout for De Niro, Warhol, and a slew of other celebs. You can still feel them in the room.

It's pretty much my office away from the office. When I get done with the show and whatever other nonsense I have to take care of at the studio, I usually make a beeline for the Odeon bar. They know I'm coming.

Then there's Walker's. It's a "locals only"–type bar, a mix of off-duty cops from the precinct around the corner and old-timers who look like they've been holding down the same barstool since Ed Koch was mayor, and the fun, young crowd that appreciates its importance. Yes, celebrities wander through—but only because they live in the neighborhood. No one comes to Walker's to be seen.

There's no chrome. No neon. No fancy cocktails. It's calm and comfortable and casual. The walls have random bits of whatever on them. The chairs wobble. The tables are covered in butcher paper, and they'll bring you crayons so you can draw penises on them. And we usually do. Fun fact: Penises are the most drawn crayon art at Walker's. In second place: I'M WITH STUPID, with an arrow pointing to the right.

You can come in by yourself at eleven in the morning and sit at the bar and nurse a glass of wine and enjoy some really great pasta and think about life. Or you can come in with a group of friends and crowd around the table in back and order tequila shots and sing along to the music. Either way, by the second time you come in, you're a regular just like everybody else.

See, the key to happiness in New York is to find *your* one percent—the six-block radius that contains everything you truly need. The bodega where they know to put extra hot sauce on your egg sandwich. The diner where they're always playing amazing Motown songs. The bar that has your drink poured before your butt hits the chair. The Walgreens that's open twenty-four hours for late-night milk and toilet paper runs.

And, of course, it's not just places that matter. It's people, too. The old lady (wearing too much lipstick and a fake fur) down the block who's out walking her even older dog at exactly the same time every morning. The guy in the apartment building across the street who always forgets to pull down the shades while he walks around with his saggy old-man junk dragging on the floor. The construction workers who've been working at digging the same hole for what feels like years.

Walker's is great, but there are a million different places you could go to get shitfaced in this city. What makes Walker's *Walker's*—what made it the first place in the city where I ever felt like I was home—is the people. Like Steven, the big Southern belle of a waiter who's lived in New York as long as I have but somehow managed to keep his accent. And Leonard, the famous bartender who's been holding court and telling stories since, I don't know, the invention of alcohol.

And then, of course, there's Linda. Well, it's not pronounced "Linda." It's pronounced "Linder." She insists.

Anyway, Linda has been around Tribeca forever and a day. She's cool and funny and laid-back, and she has a heart as big as Manhattan. She refuses to let anyone in her bar feel like a stranger for long. Linda's seen everything and everyone, but the only way to impress her is to be a nice person and have that karmic "warmth" that she loves. The day I got her seal of approval was the day I felt like I'd earned my New York City card. She's always brutally honest and tells it like it is. No nonsense. No bullshit.

Linda's a big believer in the power of the cosmos. Not Cosmopolitans. The Universe. The first, oh, thousand or so times I came in the door, she'd spot me from across the room and yell, "I knew you'd be coming in today!" Well, yeah, no shit, Linda—I'm here almost every day. But then one day I came in and she looked up in shock. "I had no idea you'd be here today!" So maybe she isn't full of shit after all.

It's funny. When you move from market to market like radio people tend to do, you get used to setting up a new "family" in every town. You stock your life with friends and romantic interests and bartenders knowing that in a few months you're going to ghost them all. I always think that's what it must be like for actors who work together on a movie set or a TV show. For as long as you're there, those people are so important to you. You see them every day. You share everything. You see each other at your most intimate. And then one day the director calls a wrap, and you all move on.

I never expected to settle down anywhere. I'm used to treating many seemingly important things as disposable. Even in New York, where I've been for almost thirty years, I think of my apartment less as a home and more as a really nice hotel suite. It's where my stuff is. But it's not where my heart is. My heart is in the people I've met here. The family I've built here.

I always feel a spiritual connection with listeners who are NYC to their bones. I love hearing a heavy New York accent on the street, or talking to New York City cops and firefighters who remind me of the heroism and pride we continue to see long after 9/11, or just listening to people argue about where to get the best slice of pizza.

But I also feel a connection with New York transplants like myself. People who came from somewhere they didn't quite fit in the hopes that the greatest city in the world would be big enough for them to find a place of their own.

I think we all sometimes feel stuck in the wrong place, surrounded by people who don't understand or appreciate us. But if that's you, know that you're not stuck at all. You're just on a journey and haven't reached your destination yet.

Because the truth is, we don't get to decide where we're born. But we do get to decide where home is. We don't get to decide what our parents are like. But we do get to decide who our family is.

New York is where I made a home and found a family. And even if my journey takes me somewhere else, I'll love this big, crazy, smelly city forever.

Or at least I'll always have Walker's.

CHAPTER 9

Bad Advice from an
Accidental Media Mogul

I sometimes show up for work at the same time as Charlamagne Tha God, who does the morning show down the hall at Power 105.1.

I love walking to work when I can. But Charlamagne does not get to experience that little joy. And not just because he lives outside the city. He spends four hours a day trying to challenge and provoke his audience, and sometimes that means pissing people off. So the other twenty hours of the day, people often want to challenge him back.

That's why *he* comes to work in a black SUV along with two or three huge guys whose job it is to make sure he gets into the building safely. Think he's paranoid? Think again. One morning, the SUV pulled up just as I was arriving, and some random guy popped up out of nowhere and started screaming at him. I watched from a safe distance while Wax, his linebacker-size body man, carefully stepped in front of Charlamagne, ready to kick this guy's ass if necessary. It looked like it could get ugly.

But Charlamagne himself was totally unfazed. He could have easily kept on walking, but he stopped to let this confused man say his piece. The guy's ass remained unkicked. And as we all walked through the revolving doors into the building, Charlamagne looked at me and shrugged. "See what I'm saying about mental health?" he said.

I did. I'd just been reading his latest book, *Shook One*, which is a story about how he took on his own issues and a plea for his audience to start taking mental illness seriously. I'd been amazed at how passionate he was about this one important issue. And now I was blown away by his composure. If a wild-eyed stranger jumped out of the bushes at *me* at a quarter to six in the morning, I would have pissed my pants. I would have pissed YOUR pants.

There's a lot about Charlamagne that makes me shake my head in awe. It always feels like he knows exactly what he wants and how to get it—and he isn't going to let *anything* stand in his way. He grew up tough. He served time in jail for dealing drugs. He's gone through shit I can't even imagine. But here he is, on top of the world. Radio. TV. Books. He's always planning out his next move. Nothing shakes him. Never bet against someone with that kind of drive and focus and work ethic. I know I wouldn't.

That's something I've noticed about a lot of my peers who started in radio and have gone on to conquer the media universe. Like my friend Bobby Bones. I don't get how he makes time for stuff like *American Idol* and *Dancing with the Stars* on top of doing his show every day. Plus, he sings in a band that tours the country! By the time I get to 10 a.m., I'm done. Or Ryan Seacrest.

That guy is *everywhere*! He's probably going to launch another new show by the time I finish this sentence.

These guys aren't just hosts. They're whole *industries*. And they're always working harder and harder to come up with new ways to reach new audiences.

Not me. I'm an *awful* time manager. I'm the most disorganized person in the world. My apartment is full of boxes. I have no idea what's in half of them. I love starting projects, but I suck at finishing them. Just getting to the end of a season of a TV show, I feel like I deserve a trophy and a parade.

Maybe I'm afraid of commitment. Or maybe I just hate the idea of spending any more time on work than I absolutely have to.

Which, by the way, is a really bad trait to have if you want to write a book. Charlamagne and Bobby have each written two, and I have no idea how they made it look so easy. This is a nightmare! I mean, I love telling these stories. But actually *writing* this fucking thing? What an unbelievable pain in the ass. I can't tell you how many hours—days!—I've spent wandering around my apartment in sweatpants, dreading having to actually pound away on my Mac. I bet Ryan Seacrest doesn't even *own* sweatpants.

Alex always makes fun of me when I complain about how hard my life is. He'll come home and ask me what I want to do for dinner. "I don't feel like going out," I'll say.

"You want to cook?"

"Nah. I'm pretty wiped. Let's order in."

He always rolls his eyes at that. "You go to work and push buttons and talk for two hours, and then you leave," he'll say.

"Yeah," I always reply, "and look what they pay me!"

The thing is, Alex doesn't understand what it takes to do a

daily radio show. I describe it as like sitting in an electric chair for several hours a day. I'm surrounded by total chaos while having to have my head in the game at all times. Remember, we're not reading scripts. It's all controlled confusion.

And I do love it. But I love being at home even more.

You could offer me a free trip on the space shuttle, in first class, with complimentary drink service, but if it meant leaving the house on a weeknight, I'd have to think about it. I'd probably wind up canceling at the last minute. "Um, yeah, I can't go to Mars today, I think I'm coming down with something."

I *love* doing nothing. When I open the calendar on my phone and see big, empty white spaces, it's like getting a massage. On the other hand, if I see a notification pop up about something my assistant has put on my schedule? I practically break out in hives. My life is a constant battle against *doing shit.*

If my allergy to extra work bothers Alex, it *really* bothers my agent, David Katz. David is a brilliant guy who loves the entertainment business. He is so supportive, and he's always trying to get me to try different things and add new tricks to my bag so I can expand my reach in the entertainment world, or at least make more money. But it's hopeless.

In fairness, I did *try* to follow his advice. Once. This was way back when I was doing afternoons at Z100. I was bored enough to actually try something new, and so I picked the thing that sounded like it would involve the least amount of work: voice-overs. I figured, I manage to spend four hours a day talking into a microphone. What's another few minutes?

David found me an audition and sent me an address.

One problem. Twice a year, every year, pollen just completely overtakes New York, and I totally lose my voice. And, of course, I woke up that morning with nothing. But I went to the studio in some shitty building in a shitty neighborhood. I got buzzed in, and I guess I was early, because the lady who worked there was just getting things set up. I walked in with a polite smile on my face and started to introduce myself, but she cut me off. "For God's sake, just sit out in the hallway and wait for me to get ready. You know how this works!"

Uh, no, I didn't. But okay. "No problem," I croaked. I sounded as if I was going through puberty. She shot me a weird look.

A few minutes later: "Elvis?" I walked in, pretty sure I'd already blown it. "Okay," she said, pointing to the mic. "You're playing the part of a weatherman on a news talk radio station." She handed me the copy, and I started squeaking away into the mic. I got about fifteen seconds in before she cut me off.

"What's wrong with your voice?" she demanded.

"Uh, I lost it."

She shook her head. "Lemme ask you something. You came all the way down here in the pouring rain and waited to audition, but you have no voice. How exactly did you think you were gonna get this job?"

The best I could come up with was, "Because I'm a great person?" She didn't seem amused.

"Thank you. Next!"

I walked out and no one was there. I was the only person who had shown up for the audition. And I didn't get it.

With David's encouragement, I tried just a *little* bit harder.

When I got my voice back, I put together a tape showcasing my skills, and he sent it out. One day, David called me and said, "Okay, I got you something. It's a TV spot. They heard the tape, and they think you'd match."

"Match *what*?"

"Just go."

Okay. So I went to the studio. Much nicer than the other one. It was run by this older guy.

"Here's the deal," he said. "We did this TV commercial, but we don't like the guy's voice who plays the lead character. We want you to dub over his lines in your voice."

"You want me to lip-synch?" I asked.

"Exactly. You've done this, right?"

"I've never done this in my life," I said.

The guy shrugged. "You'll be great." Then he explained the premise of the commercial: It's about a small-business owner who owns a bike shop. And he's talking about how he got a loan from this bank, and how great the experience was. (Apparently, the bank was in the South, and so they'd picked me because of my drawl.)

Got it. So he pushed play, and then, all of a sudden—hey! The actor was someone I knew! Actually, he was someone I'd worked with during the few months I'd spent down in Atlanta.

"Hey, I know that guy," I said. "How weird is that? I'm gonna be dubbing my voice over Mike's? So weird!"

The guy couldn't have cared less. "Uh-huh. Just get in the booth, put the headphones on, and try to match his lips."

I got about half a sentence in. "You know, when I was first looking for a small-business loan from First Republic Bank, I—"

"STOP!" he yelled from the other side of the glass. "You sound like an announcer. You need to sound like a guy who owns a fucking bike shop. Try it again."

"You know, when I was first looking for a small-business—"

"CUT!" The guy pounded the button to talk into my headphones with a closed fist. "You're not listening to me! You sound like a fucking announcer. Just sound like a guy with a bike shop."

I couldn't believe how belligerent he was *already* getting. "Well," I said, trying to be polite, "maybe the problem is that you recorded the actor outdoors with a little clip-on microphone. I'm in this studio with professional recording equipment. The acoustics are totally different."

He slammed the button again. "I've been doing this for thirty years. You don't know what the *fuck* you're talking about!" This guy was getting *really* mad. "Try it again!"

At this point, I was sweating bullets. Take three, no good. Take four, no good. Take five, no good. "You're not matching his lips at all!" I heard the engineer in the background telling the guy he could probably fix it in postproduction. But I think it was personal now.

The more takes I did, the more irritated the guy got. He was *mean*. And at some point it dawned on me that I didn't really need to be doing this. I *had* a regular job on Z100. This gig barely paid anything anyway. I was only here because I was bored.

So, after a few more "CUT!"s and a few more "TRY IT AGAIN, ASSHOLE!"s, I took off my headphones. "Let me just go get a glass of water. I'll be right back, and I'll get it right." And then I walked out the door, with zero intention of coming right back, or of coming back *ever*. I wish I could remember that guy's name so I could put it in this book. What a dick.

As soon as I could get to a phone, I called David. "This mother-fucker," I sputtered. "How could you set me up with someone like that?"

David just laughed. "I guess you don't really want to do voice-over," he said.

Here's the kicker: I *got the job.* I can only imagine how bad all the other auditions had to have been for them to want me after all that.

That brings me to the big piece of advice I have to share in this chapter. And I'm kind of worried that it's actually shitty advice.

See, books like this one always have great advice designed to motivate readers. *Here's how to overcome your fears! Here's how to hurdle obstacles! Here's how to become the world-conquering ass-kicker you've always wanted to be!*

I wish I could help you with that. But I can't. I keep reading books like *The 7 Habits of Highly Effective People* and *How to Win Friends and Influence People,* and I get super-inspired, and then five minutes later I'm back to watching the Food Network and wishing I could beat Bobby Flay.

So, my advice is really more of a question: Are you sure you actually *do* want to conquer the world?

Don't get me wrong. I respect the hell out of "successful" people who are constantly pushing themselves to achieve more and more. People who will get to do things I'll never even come close to doing.

But I don't *envy* them. Not even for one second. I could never be Ryan Seacrest, not just because he's got better hair and teeth than I do, but because I don't *want* that kind of success enough to do the work it takes to get it. I don't want to be the king of all media. I want to do a great radio show every day, and then I want to go home and drink a glass of wine and read a book. And if you think that sounds lazy, well, you're welcome to that voice-over job.

See, to me, being happy isn't about turning yourself into the person you wish you could be. It's about building the life that fits the person you *are*. And to do that, you have to get to *know* that person. You have to know the difference between what you truly love and what you only think you like. You have to know what you're naturally good at, and what you're willing to work hard to get better at, and what you're just never going to learn. And you have to be at peace with it so you can focus on finding the thing that allows you to be the best version of yourself.

I mean, I'm really good at talking on the radio. And I always want to get better. But there's a lot of stuff about myself I'm never going to bother to "work on."

For example: I'm super impatient. Anything I want, I want it *now*, like that mean girl from *Charlie and the Chocolate Factory*. I want my fucking Oompa Loompa NOW! I hate waiting in lines. And I'm impatient with *people*, too. I can't stand when people don't understand what I'm trying to tell them. Why can't everyone just read my mind?

So, I could try really hard to become more patient. Maybe more meditating. Or smoking more weed. But instead, I just deal with the fact that patience is a gift I don't have. And I work around it.

Also, I hate shitty hotels. I know that makes me a snob. I'm not sorry. That's just who I am.

People who give relationship advice are really into *understanding* and *acceptance*. And yeah, you have to understand and accept your partner. There's that romantic-comedy trope about trying to "change" someone into the person you want him or her to be. It never works, right?

But you know what else never works? Trying to change *yourself* into a different person you don't need to be. If you want to be happy, I think you have to start by understanding who you are—and accepting yourself.

That's probably terrible advice if you're hoping to take over the world someday. But I think it's good advice if you want to enjoy the life you actually have.

And, by the way, I'm not telling you to settle for the life you have if you don't enjoy it, or if you think you could enjoy it more. If you want to lose weight or learn a new skill or meet that special someone, by all means, get out there and work for what you want. But the Universe has a way of guiding us toward the things we were *meant* to do. If something that feels like hard work for everybody else seems to come naturally to you, then maybe that's what you're wired for. Own it!

Being jealous of other people, or of some imaginary life you wish you had, is a waste. Instead, use that time and energy to figure out what it is that makes you feel like the best version of yourself. To use old-school radio terms: We all broadcast at a different frequency. Don't be afraid to scan the dial until you find yours.

Refusing to give a shit about the things you aren't passionate about means you have plenty of shits left to give about the things you *do* care about. All that time I'm not out hustling is time I get to spend with the people I love, in the places I love, enjoying the things I love. And the energy I don't devote to becoming a bigger star is energy I can spend doing a better show.

See, along with bad hotel rooms, another pet peeve of mine is when things don't live up to their potential. The way I see it, either do something *right*, or don't do it at all. There's just way too much TV to watch to waste time and energy doing a half-assed job of anything.

For those four hours I'm on the air, I will run through a brick wall to make our show the best it can be. And yeah, I'll push myself. After Elliot left, I could have just let the show slowly circle the drain until we got canceled. And it took a lot to steer it onto a new course. I had to trust my gut. I had to piss off my coworkers. I had to take a risk. But I didn't want to just do a watered-down version of the same old show. And I knew it was worth fighting to make sure the show reached its potential.

After 9/11, I got an even clearer picture of what that potential really was. We *weren't* just about goofy jokes. We were in the business of serving our listeners—and, on a day like that or on any random Tuesday, the service we provided could make a huge difference in their lives. I was dead set on doing whatever it took to make sure we lived up to the standard we set that day.

Of course, with the show at number one in New York, we needed to find new frontiers to explore. And I wasn't interested in giving the voice-over stuff another go. The logical next step was syndication.

Syndication is like the holy grail for radio shows. It means a bigger audience, a bigger footprint—and, okay, a bigger paycheck. But it's not just about money or ego. The more markets you're in, and the more people who are listening, the more you can do with the show.

Several contracts ago, I'd gotten the right to syndicate my own show by offering it to other stations around the country, which is a "deal point" (David's term) not many radio hosts get. It's a Howard Stern–level privilege. But we'd agreed to give (then owner) Clear Channel's syndication division, Premiere Radio Networks, first crack at syndicating the show for us—after all, they were the pros.

But they weren't interested. When we went to the president of Premiere, Charlie Rahilly, he told us our show was too New York—that no one outside the area would be interested in such a "local" show.

That didn't make any sense to me. I mean, sure, listeners in Seattle probably didn't care about the traffic on the Tappan Zee Bridge. But I'd lived all over the country, and I was pretty sure New Yorkers aren't the only people who like to wake up in the morning and laugh and be entertained. Did they really believe that nobody else in the country wanted to talk about entertainment and relationships and whether candy corn is delicious or disgusting?

Finally, in 2006, we got Tom Poleman to agree to put us on Z100's sister station in Miami: Y100. Miami is like the sixth borough of New York. Unless you count Puerto Rico. So maybe it's the seventh. Either way, our show would get a chance to fill Y100's morning drive-time slot every day.

But we were on probation from day one. Tom warned us that

the company was scared about putting us on in another market. We were number one in New York, and adding an affiliate could dilute the success we were having. So we did something insane: We agreed that if our ratings dropped in New York, we'd pull ourselves off the air in Miami. It was a risk no one in their right mind would take. But we believed in the show.

Besides, I was so excited. I've always loved Miami. And adding the market gave us a boost of energy to reinvent the show—and a great excuse to spend more time on the beach.

I took a trip down to South Florida to meet with station management and get the lay of the land, and that's where I met one of the Y100 morning-show hosts, a guy named Froggy. The first time I met him, we took a helicopter tour of the area together, and I just loved the guy right away. In fact, I had a great idea.

The management at Y100 was understandably skeptical about us coming in. They thought we didn't play enough music, and they didn't think the music we played would work for the Miami audience. We had a lot of early battles where they didn't want to give up total control of their airwaves and we refused to let them mess with our show.

But what if we could make it feel less like a takeover and more like a merger? What if Froggy became part of our crew? Yeah, it would be weird at first, having someone on the show we couldn't see (later, we'd get video cameras set up so we could see Froggy sitting in front of his mic down in Miami). We needed someone on the ground there to help us make this actually work.

I was confident he'd fit right in with us, and I thought it would be a great way to bridge the distance between New York and South Florida.

Actually, it's not even that far! A quick nonstop flight. In the winter, I'd spend weeks at a time broadcasting from the studio in Miami. It would be cold and snowy in New York—the streets would be covered with that gray slush that gets up in your pant legs—and we'd be walking out of the studio in shorts and sunglasses, ready to spend the afternoon by the pool at the beautiful Acqualina Resort & Spa. Sometimes we'd all go. Sometimes it would be just me and Froggy, with everyone else stuck back in New York. Turns out you can do a radio show from anywhere.

Even better: Our insane risk paid off. We busted our asses to do a better show. Sharper bits. Tighter breaks. More character development. More energy. More fun. And not only did our ratings in New York not tank, they went up by more than 20 percent.

I thought that with Miami a success, it wouldn't be long before Premiere picked us up for national syndication. I was daydreaming about going on the air in all the markets I'd been fired in before, and even some I *hadn't* been fired in! But we kept waiting and waiting and being told to wait some more. It felt like every week someone *else* was getting syndicated—getting the opportunity I felt like we'd earned. More wasted potential.

The final straw came the day I found out that Premiere had given Whoopi Goldberg a national syndication deal for her brandnew morning show, *Wake Up with Whoopi*. Nothing against Whoopi herself, but *come on*. I'd been on top in New York for several years, and Whoopi had never even hosted a show before. Now, all of a sudden, they were putting her on in something like eight of the top ten markets in the country.

Fuck that. The day I got the news about Whoopi's show, I decided that if the bosses weren't going to let our show reach its full potential, I didn't want to do it at all. I stomped out of the studio, got in my car, and started driving out to Pottersville.

I was almost to the farmhouse when I got a call from Gene Romano, one of the programming directors at the company. "What are you *doing*?" he asked me.

I was in no mood to talk. "You can all go fuck yourselves," I told Gene.

Fortunately, Gene was used to "talent fits" like the one I was throwing. He wasn't happy, but he managed to stay calm. "Elvis," he said, "if you want to be syndicated, you have to do it the right way."

Apparently throwing a temper tantrum and storming out of work didn't count as "the right way." I was almost back in Pottersville, land of no cell service, so I pulled over to the side of the road and let Gene keep talking. He explained that if the company simply forced program directors at stations across the country to put our show on, they'd have to do it, but they wouldn't really support us. We'd be destined to fail.

I was still pissed. But I knew Gene was right. "Okay," I said. "I'll come to work tomorrow."

I've never been afraid to walk away from a job, even my dream job, if I couldn't do it the right way. My way. Negotiating contracts is always kind of a high-wire act. I hate it. Things have always gone well with the current leadership team at iHeartMedia (hi, guys—love you!), but every time my contract comes up, I'm ready to be unemployed if things don't go my way.

It's not the money that hangs us up. I just don't want to do anything other than *my* show, *my* way. And I care about that principle so much, I'm willing to lose everything for it. I have enough saved up that I could go buy a place in some small town somewhere. I'd get the kitchen redone so I could cook. And I'd buy another DIY studio so I could do a show every day, the way I want it. Even if I'm back to an audience of just me and the next-door neighbors.

This is also probably bad advice, by the way. I don't recommend treating every negotiation with your bosses as a blowup waiting to happen. But I can only be who I am.

Fortunately, when it came to syndication, there was another option between getting what I wanted and barricading myself inside the farmhouse in New Jersey, refusing to take anyone's calls: We could do what Howard Stern had done and syndicate the show ourselves.

That's when David really stepped up to the plate. After a long career at Don Buchwald & Associates (ironically, Don is Howard's agent)—and many years of pleading with me to take my own career more seriously—David left to become my business partner. We founded what we called the Elvis Duran Group, and David started shopping the show to radio stations around the country.

I'd never been a CEO before. Remember, I didn't even like being a *manager*. But I actually enjoyed figuring out how to make this new arrangement work for our show. We took half the staff and put them on the Elvis Duran Group payroll, which made Clear Channel happy. And we took a new approach to dealing with program directors in the different stations we were pitching.

In Miami, we'd had trouble agreeing on a playlist that would work for both markets. And when we were looking for new stations to take the show, we kept hearing that same concern. After one conversation with a program director, we had an idea. Instead of playing everything from New York, we'd take regular nine-minute breaks where individual stations could play local commercials, promos—and whatever music their hearts desired. If we timed it out right, it would be seamless: Listeners would never know that the rock song they were hearing in, say, Des Moines wasn't the song people were hearing in New York.

Before long, we'd signed on two more big markets: Philly and Cleveland. It felt great. We were doing it *our* way. We gave our employees really nice cash bonuses. We came up with cool ideas and didn't have to ask anyone's permission to do them. Once, we flew the whole show to London for a week's worth of broadcasts, just because.

Then came time for my next round of contract negotiations. Clear Channel had just brought in a new CEO, Bob Pittman—a longtime showbiz guy who had worked at places like MTV and Time Warner—and he called me uptown for a meeting.

I *hate* meetings. Even more than that, I *hate* going uptown. Which, in my map of the city, is anywhere north of the Village. I know there's lots of great stuff up there. I don't care. The traffic alone is enough to keep me down in Tribeca. Especially during the holidays. Holy *shit*. The scene outside Rockefeller Center? Total nightmare. I'm getting itchy just thinking about sitting in a car, trying to make it through those crowds.

But *this* trip uptown turned out to be worth it. Bob explained that the company needed to reduce its costs, especially in smaller markets, and that it was planning to do more syndication. "Wouldn't it be easier," he said, "if we had all your employees under our umbrella, and we just went ahead and syndicated you nationally?"

Victory is mine!

Today, a decade later, we're on in eighty markets, and I know every single one, because there's a big map in my office with a picture of my face pinned to everywhere we're on.

We haven't clicked in every market, of course. When we tried to bring our show to Richmond, Virginia, people picketed the station, upset about the local show being displaced. In Lancaster, Pennsylvania—Amish country!—someone wrote an angry newspaper column about how we were just big-city devils coming to corrupt the youth. Which wasn't *entirely* untrue. But once we'd been on for a while, the same guy wrote another piece acknowledging that we weren't so bad after all. In fact, we made it to number one in Lancaster.

We're number one in a lot of places now. The same people who once doubted our success now take credit for putting us on. And you know what? I don't even feel like saying, "I told you so."

Okay, maybe just once: *I told you so!*

So how is it that the same guy who bailed on his voice-over career after one and a half auditions stuck with the syndication project until he made it work?

Simple: This radio show is *my thing*. It's where all my professional desire and focus are concentrated. It's the only thing I care about enough to work hard at. And, to be honest with you, most days, it doesn't even feel like *work*.

I'm lucky that I found *my thing* very early in life. Maybe this isn't the same for you. I talk to a lot of callers who thought they had found *their thing*. But trying to reach the goals they've set for themselves feels like slogging through quicksand every day. Maybe that sounds more like your life. Maybe you went to medical school because both your parents are doctors, but you hate going to class. Maybe you've always wanted to write a book, but you keep getting stuck on the first chapter (this one, I can identify with).

I'm not here to tell you that you should up and quit. But keep an open mind. Because I really do believe there's something out there for everybody. And that includes you. There's something out there that really *is* your thing. Something that you can pour your whole self into and it won't feel like work. Something you're ready to fight for. Could be a job. Could be a family. Could be windsurfing.

It might not be the thing you think it is. And it might not be the thing everybody else expects of you. It's weird to say, but I think you don't get to *decide* who you are. You have to *find out*. And the sooner you do, the happier you'll be.

Charlamagne, Bobby Bones, Ryan Seacrest—they're good friends and great talents. But I'm not them. I'm just me. And I wouldn't want it any other way.

How I Met Your Father
(In Case We Ever Have Kids)

One Sunday morning in 2010, I woke up in Miami, not knowing that my boring social life back in New York was about to wake up. I reached for my phone and saw a Facebook friend request from a famous groundhog named Staten Island Chuck.

And that's how I met the man who would one day be my husband.

Of course, if you're a regular listener to my show, you already know about Alex. In fact, you've probably gotten to know him pretty well. I talk about him all the time. Sometimes I'll even call him on his cell phone to get him to weigh in on something during the show.

Back when I was young and reckless (as opposed to middle-aged and reckless), I never would have imagined getting married. Or, for that matter, living in a world where I *could* get married. And I never would have imagined that I'd be sharing all the details—everything from the proposal to the wedding planning— with millions of people on the radio.

So, this is MY story of how Alex and I got together. But it's also the story of how, after years of keeping my personal life personal, I finally opened up and let the whole world in.

I certainly didn't mind people knowing I was gay. Everybody at work knew. All my friends knew. Even my parents knew, even if we never talked about it.

But just like I never officially "came out" to Mom and Dad, I had never really "come out" to my radio audience. There'd never been a dramatic announcement. I hadn't done the soft-focus sit-down interview. I wasn't hiding anything. I just didn't talk about my personal life on the air.

In part, that was because I didn't want to be defined by it the way Ellen DeGeneres had been. When she came out on her (now defunct) sitcom in 1997, it was an unbelievable landmark moment. I thought she was a hero. But I also noticed that, for a while, she was seen as "Ellen, the Out Lesbian." She's so talented and funny, but it took some time before her sexuality stopped being the first thing people thought about when they saw her on TV.

Of course, all this seems a little dated now. Thanks to Ellen and a bunch of other pioneers, it's no longer a big deal for a media figure to come out. But this is now, and that was then, and even if I didn't feel shy about my sexuality, I knew that people would be curious.

And the thing was, I didn't want to be known as "Elvis Duran, the Gay DJ." More important, I didn't want our show to be the "Elvis Duran Is Gay" show. Our whole thing was that our show was for *everybody.*

If I'm being honest, though, keeping my personal life private only had so much to do with being gay. Truth is, while I'd gotten pretty good at *asking* people probing questions about their innermost thoughts and feelings, I'd never really been comfortable answering them. What's up with that? As I learned, most interviewers HATE being interviewed.

Either way, for a long time, I never talked about my dating life on the air. Which meant my audience never really got to know the guy I was with for several years in my early forties. Which is probably for the best, because the story didn't exactly have a happy ending. Not going to get into specifics. We simply weren't meant to be together.

The breakup was long and painful. I spent a good amount of time in therapy trying to sort out how to get out of it with the least amount of damage—to both of us. It wasn't easy. But we managed.

New single me. New single life. I stopped hiding out at the farmhouse in Pottersville and moved back to NYC. The ultimate destination for a middle-aged single man.

The idea behind buying a place in Manhattan had been that if I spent a few nights there a week, I could cut down on my commute and sleep in a bit instead of waking up in the middle of the night to drive in from New Jersey. The flip side of that, of course, is that when you live in New York City, there's always something exciting going on, and more often than not, you wind up staying *out* until the middle of the night.

That's especially true when you're coming off a bad breakup and diving headfirst back into the dating game. I'd been a single guy in the city before, and now it was time to truly enjoy my midlife crisis. I was really embracing it. If you're gonna get tacky about it, go all the way! I had money in the bank, a job I loved, and a liver that still functioned. New York became my playground.

There was a time when I became semiserious with a younger guy. Okay, a *lot* younger. *Okay*, he was twenty-one. Don't judge me. We had a *ton* of fun. We would party late, go home, and stay up later . . . a few nights going, until the alarm went off for a new day of work.

I was really leaning into the wild and crazy. I even bought a new car—a top-of-the-line Porsche 911. They delivered it right to my apartment, and the moment it arrived, my young friend and I hopped in and drove it straight to Atlantic City at two hundred miles an hour (or at least that's how I remember it). There were cocktails and more cocktails, and at some point somebody reminded me that I was supposed to introduce my friend Jason Derulo onstage at the Borgata (oh yeah, *that's* why I was in Atlantic City!), and I somehow made it through that without falling over, and then there were more cocktails, and then Jason suggested a round of shots, and, what, were we going to say no to that?

At some point, I found myself at one of those high-roller slot machines, feeding it hundred-dollar bills while I pounded complimentary drinks. Somehow, I kept winning . . . and winning . . . and winning. The kind of winning where they have to send over a manager to pay you. Before long—I swear, this story is true—I had won thousands. *Tens* of thousands. I couldn't keep track of it all. I was sloppy, giddy, tequila spilling on my shirt and cash spilling out of my pockets. Someone eventually went over to the Old Homestead Steakhouse to get a to-go bag, and we filled it to the brim with what we later realized was more than sixty thousand dollars in slot winnings. We had a room upstairs, and someone dragged me into the elevator, cash blowing everywhere.

Cut to: the next morning. At least I hadn't imagined the big bag of money. And so we did the only thing we could: hopped right back into the Porsche and raced back up the Garden State Parkway. We drove so fast the temporary plates blew off. I can only imagine what would have happened if we'd run into a state trooper—no plates, big sack of hundred-dollar bills, probably still a bit buzzed from the night before. When we pulled over for gas, I realized I had no idea where the gas tank was on a Porsche. We eventually had to call someone to ask.

Anyway, I was having a great time. And I was racking up a lot of fun stories, the kind you invite all your friends to brunch just to tell. But then I'd go to work every morning, and I'd hop on the mic to talk to my millions of friends out in the world, and . . . I wouldn't tell them. It started to feel wrong. Our show was all about being open and honest. People appreciated feeling like they really *knew* us. And here I was, only telling a small part of my story. Maybe . . . because I needed more in my life to be proud about.

So, one day, without planning to do it or meaning to do it or even really noticing that I *was* doing it, I came out on the radio. It wasn't an "announcement," exactly. I just happened to mention it in response to a caller.

And then something amazing happened. *Nobody cared.*

Well, that's not quite right. I did get some supportive messages from friends and listeners, and that was nice. I also heard from a few young gay kids who felt more empowered to be open about who *they* were, and that was *really* nice.

But for the most part, the reaction from the world was basically: "Oh, you're gay? Cool. What else is going on?"

I think I had always imagined that it would be this seismic moment, like when Ellen came out. But—in large part *because* of Ellen's courage and the courage of people like her—the day I came out was just another day at the office.

I know it isn't like that for everyone. A lot of people who are thinking about coming out worry that their parents or their friends or their coworkers will give them a hard time. And unfortunately, sometimes that does happen. It can be the most brutal time in a person's life.

But whenever I'm asked about it, I always suggest to young gay men and women that maybe, just maybe, it won't be as hard as they think. It is *never* a bad idea to live your truth—to be who you are and be *proud* of who you are. And by the way, "who you are" is more than your sexuality. It's the music you love, and your sense of humor, and the way you always stop to pet other people's dogs. The people who love you love a *lot* of things about you. You should be prepared for the possibility that coming out will turn out to be the best gift you can give yourself.

And yeah, you may run into some bullies. But if you surround yourself with people who love and accept you, the way I have with my radio family and my New York family and my audience family, those assholes will just get drowned out by all the supportive voices who are thrilled to see you owning another piece of your identity. Rainbows as far as the eye can see! Too gay?

*　　*　　*

This all sounds pretty wise coming from a guy who just a decade ago was afraid to say anything about his personal life on the air. I guess I've done some learning as I've gotten older and grayer. And maybe coming out was part of a process of growing up that I needed to go through before I could be ready for the kind of relationship I'm in today.

Which brings me back to that groundhog.

Staten Island Chuck is a local institution. He emerges from his Staten Island Zoo bunker every February 2 to predict the weather, and we would typically send Greg T to cover the big event live. But, that fateful Sunday morning in Miami, I couldn't figure out why I'd gotten a friend request from what appeared to be an animated GIF of a famous rodent.

Then I got a second friend request—this one from an actual human being named Alex Carr. He looked cute, as far as I could tell from the tiny photo.

I did what anyone would do: I googled him. Turned out he was a zookeeper at the Staten Island Zoo. *Aha.* Putting two and two together, I sent him a message asking if he had anything to do with the groundhog. Indeed, he confirmed. Now this was getting interesting. *Commence cyberstalking!*

I found some higher-resolution pictures, and he was even cuter in those. Plus, he had an interesting job in a totally different field from mine. (Good idea. Radio guys are weird.) And as we sent messages back and forth, I discovered that he was a lot of fun to chat with. I even figured out that I was friends with his cousin Anthony. (As it turns out, Anthony wasn't his real cousin. It's one of those Staten Island things where everyone is your "cousin" and everyone is named Anthony. Don't ask.)

I started to get that "something is happening here" tingle. One day, we made the big move from Facebook chat to texting. And after a few weeks of that, Alex sent a text inviting me to hang out with him—*in person!*—the next evening.

But that was a pretty high-stakes ask. The next night was going to be the Wednesday before Thanksgiving, also known as the world's most underrated party night. In fact, I'd already been invited to a gathering at a friend's house. But I texted him back that I'd meet him for a drink beforehand.

Great, he replied. *Meet me at the Monster?*

Ugh. The Monster is a legendary gay bar in New York, but not one of my favorites. I'd only been there once, years before, and the crowd had been kind of old—REALLY old. Still, I was interested enough that I figured I could put up with the Monster for a little while on the way to my friend's house.

The next morning, I did something very old-fashioned: I called Alex, on the telephone, to confirm.

"Hey," I said when he picked up. "It's Elvis."

"Oh, hey," he said. "We still on for tonight?"

Remember: This was the first time I'd ever heard his voice. So it was also the first time I realized that Alex had that *ridiculous* Staten Island accent that I loved. Seriously, he sounded like something out of a movie. *Oh my God*, I thought.

Then I found out that Alex, who I later learned was really nervous about meeting me, was coming with backup. "Yeah," he said, "I'll be there with my friends Reptile Matt, Drunk Jimmy, and Uncle Johnny." Who the hell were *those* people? Did I hear him say "*Uncle* Johnny"? "Drunk Jimmy"? Was this going to be a meeting of the fuckin' Gambino crime family?

To be honest, the call didn't exactly fill me with optimism about the date. But I went anyway. And as soon as I walked into the bar and saw Alex sitting with his friends, I was hooked. He was charming and funny and even better-looking in person. He was also ultra-shy and could barely look me in the eye. And as for those friends I had been so worried about? They turned out to be a riot.

Which brings me to Uncle Johnny.

He's a *character* in the truest sense of the word, the kind of person you can't believe actually exists in real life—but that you always feel lucky you got to actually *meet*.

I'd say I have no idea how to even start describing him, but if you've heard one of his frequent appearances on our show, you know that he has his own theme song that does the job pretty well by focusing on his three most important attributes: "He's old, he's gay, and he wears a toupee!"

I noticed all three right away that first night. How could I not? Johnny knows he stands out in a crowd, and he's proud of it. I have no idea how old he actually is—I'd guess late seventies?— but I know that I'll be lucky to look half as good or have half as much fun when I'm his age.

But Johnny's not just a cartoon. I quickly realized that he was the kind of person who could instantly make not just your night but your whole life a lot more fun. At one point, he went over to the piano to sing "What a Wonderful World," and, I kid you not, he sounded *exactly* like Louis Armstrong. It brought a tear to my eye. As it turns out, Johnny can't sing ANY song unless it's in Louis Armstrong's voice. It's some strange wiring in his brain. I dunno.

The more I got to know Johnny, the more I wanted to hang out with him. He's one of those people who have so many stories that *anything* you hear about them just might be true. For example: Apparently, he used to be a male escort (he may have even gone on a "date" or two with Merv Griffin back in the day), but he was bad at it, because he would always buy his clients drinks instead of THEM buying HIS drinks. Bad business!

Among his other feats, Johnny is responsible for our favorite all-purpose exclamation: "Hello, lady!" People who hear us yell it at each other all day on the radio show sometimes wonder if we got it from Jerry Lewis. But his was, "Hey, lady!" "Hello, lady!" is all Johnny. It was his catchphrase long before it was ours.

As you might have guessed, Johnny makes his living as the life of every party. He's been a bartender for more than half a century—he works at the gay bars out on Fire Island all summer and then lives off those tips for the rest of the year back in Manhattan. Check him out behind the bar at Cherry's this summer. And when he comes on the show, he brings cocktails for everyone—never mind that it's seven in the morning. When Johnny's around, it's always tequila o'clock.

But as much as we love having him on the show, there's a lot more to our friendship off the air. Alex and I have taken Johnny (and his collection of toupees) on many vacations: Africa, Vegas, Italy, Mexico, Palm Springs, Santa Fe. He serves as our official bartender all over the world, making every cocktail more delicious. Or at least stronger.

Uncle Johnny. There's no one else like him. Thank God. One's enough.

(Love you, Uncle Johnny. And this is where he always responds with "Love you more!")

*   *   *

Anyway, you can see why I wound up staying for a second drink. And then a third. And at the Monster, they mix their cocktails *extremely* strong. I did *not* make it to my friend's party.

Actually, I'm not exactly sure *what* happened that night. I know that later, Alex's boss dropped by and bought rounds. I know that we went to several other places after the Monster. I remember falling down somewhere and hitting my head. I think at one point we ended up at a steakhouse somewhere in Tribeca, where they sat us by the window. I know that because Alex's friend Reptile Matt, who had curled up underneath the table as soon as we sat down, announced that he had to pee, crawled out from under the table, walked outside, turned around, and peed right on the window we were sitting by. Were these my new friends?

We all wound up at my apartment at the end of the night, but when we got there, Alex realized he'd left his ID at one of the bars we'd been at. So he took off to find it, leaving me and his friends at my place, and then at some point I passed out.

The next morning, I woke up in bed . . . next to Alex's boss. Who, I should mention, is straight. "Um, hey," I said. "Nothing happened, right?"

"No," he said. "Definitely not."

"Okay, good." Then his phone rang. It was Matt.

"Hey," grumbled Matt, "I just woke up on someone's couch?"

Alex's boss got out of bed and opened the bedroom door, and sure enough, there was Matt, slumped on my couch, his head in his hands. At least he didn't pee on anything.

*   *   *

So that was our *first* date. There was zero doubt that there would be a second one. And a third. Over time, I learned more about Alex— about growing up on Staten Island, about the family that I now count myself lucky to be part of, about his lifelong passion for animals.

I even found out that I'd been wrong about that call being the first time we'd ever spoken. Turns out he'd actually called into the show years earlier, back in 1998, to answer a trivia question: What was the name of the guy who did the "You've got mail!" voice for AOL?

Alex, who'd been listening from his car while he commuted into the city for college, knew the answer (Elwood Edwards), but he had also told a funny story about running into Robin Williams in New York the night before. It was a fun call, and he won the prize—tickets to a Jingle Ball. Out of the hundreds of thousands of calls I've aired on Z100, I somehow remembered Alex's.

And the more we hung out, the harder I fell—for Alex himself, of course, but also for how fun and exciting (and sometimes out of control) my life always was when he was around.

One time, Alex came along with me when I went out to LA for the iHeartMusic Awards. Once I'd taken care of my professional obligations, we hit the town, starting with a visit to the Abbey, the world-famous gay bar in West Hollywood.

I was sipping on a club soda with lime, having decided to take it easy for the night—just kidding. We were all trashed, making friends and trading shots with everyone in our vicinity. I remember meeting one guy who'd just gotten out of prison, so we just HAD to make him our new bestie.

And, of course, everyone *loved* Alex. In the land of blond

models, here was this dark-haired, foul-mouthed, heavily ac-
cented New Yorker—plus he was handsome and could handle
his liquor. Or at least he could drink a lot of it. *Handling* it was
another story.

I don't know what time it was on the clock, but I knew it was
time to go. Our friend Steven and I tried to pull Alex out of his
circle of admirers, but he wasn't having any of it. He could barely
stand up, but he raised one defiant finger straight in the air and
bellowed, sounding kind of like a drunk Fred Flintstone, "Youse
two can go *fuck* yourselves!" Which got a huge round of cheers.

"Okay," I slurred. "You know where we're staying though, right?"

"You go *fuck* yourselves," he repeated, grinning. More cheers.

So we left. Back at the Peninsula Beverly Hills, I poured myself
out of the cab and crawled up to our suite and directly into bed.
I'd been there all of five minutes when I heard the key in the door.
Looking down the hallway, I saw Alex barge into the living room
and attempt to make his way to bed, pinballing off the walls while
he tried to take off his shoes and pants.

"Alex?"

He was muttering something from the doorway to the bedroom. Then: "I gotta *pee*."

Uh-oh.

Then I heard the unmistakable sound of liquid streaming onto
expensive carpet. I sprang out of bed, grabbing towels, clothes,
anything I could find, and leapt for him, clamping his dick to stop
the stream and trying to drag him toward the bathroom. There
was pee spraying everywhere: on the walls, on the marble floor
of the hallway, on me. We were slipping and sliding everywhere.
By the time I got him into the bathroom, he had peed out an

entire evening's worth of shots and beers, and there was nothing to do but laugh.

I realize that's the second story I've told about inappropriate urination in this chapter. But life with Alex never seemed sloppy or out of control the way it had back in the bad old days when I was doing too much coke in Houston. It was just *fun*. We still laugh about what we call the "Pee-ninsula" story—and, for the record, the hotel was very nice about it.

And while the crazy times got me hooked, our relationship soon came to be about something deeper. It was all about timing. Alex had met me at a moment in his life when he needed to grow up, and I'd met him at a moment when I needed to *wake* up. Over time, I started to feel like I'd found the kind of excitement I'd always been looking for. And Alex found a way to calm down A LOT without losing his sense of fun.

I think his friends saw it first. But it took me a long time to appreciate just how strong our bond had become. Then came that evening in Vienna, where we'd gone for a radio conference and some tourism. One night, we went to dinner, and—totally unsolicited and out of nowhere—Alex looked up from his schnitzel and said, "Here's what I love about you and me."

My heart skipped a beat.

"The things that I'm weak at," he continued, uncharacteristically quietly, "you're strong at. And the places where *you* have weakness, *I* have strength. Don't we just kind of fit into each other's lives perfectly?"

I just looked at him, my Staten Island party boy, thinking, *Who* are *you?* The Alex I'd met at the Monster would never have said that, or even thought it. But that night, I finally thought about how much we were growing together—and how much this relationship meant to both of us.

The next day we went to the zoo, because that's what we do when we travel: We *always* go to the zoo. Nothing particularly exciting happened that day. Nobody peed anywhere they weren't supposed to. I think we were even totally sober. But it was one of the best days we'd ever spent together, because I realized I was walking through that zoo with the person I wanted to be with for the rest of my life.

We've both done some serious growing up since we met, as have all of the friends who make our life together what it is. Except for Uncle Johnny, who, if possible, has only gotten *less* mature. When we all go on vacation together, even to this day, we sometimes have to send him to his room for a time-out.

I think it surprised some people that Alex and I stayed together. Alex's friends had warned him about dating an older guy, and some of my friends had worried that I was going to get my heart and/or liver destroyed by falling for this retired club kid, but we've found our way.

I'd never been terribly close with my parents, and had only recently become so with my brothers, but Alex is close with his family, and I soon got close to them, too. I started learning a lot about animals and supporting the zoo. Alex has always been really into politics, so I started tagging along with him to some of the fundraisers he attended for local candidates on Staten Island.

And just like I found my place in Alex's world, he found his place in mine. Unlike in previous relationships, he never minds letting me do my thing when I'm at a work event and have to be "on" instead of just hanging out with him. He gets a kick out of it when people recognize him and ask for a selfie, but I also know he's keeping an eye on me to make sure I'm not getting swallowed up by the craziness. You may think it's fun and fabulous to be the center of attention in a large crowd. I respect that it's a part of what I do for a living, but I'd always much rather be at home with Alex and Max the dog than anywhere else on earth. As a matter of fact, I always remind Alex: *No matter where I am and whatever I'm doing in this world, I would always rather be alone with you.*

When I'm with Alex, I feel more confident, more energetic—and also *safer*. Not just because he's a big guy and nobody messes with him. I feel safer because I feel free to be myself. I feel loved and accepted. I feel appreciated for who I am—for *all* of who I am.

And isn't that what relationships—all kinds of relationships—are for? When I think about every meaningful relationship in my life—my relationship with Alex, my relationship with my Z100 family, my relationship with my New York friends, my relationship with my audience—the thing that makes them work is that I'm not afraid to be honest and open.

Maybe that's a good way to know if the relationship you're in is a good one. Or maybe it's the other way around. Maybe it's that you can only find people who are going to make your life better if you're ready to share yourself with them fully and freely.

I don't know. It's complicated. But I'm glad I have a partner to explore these kinds of questions with. And I'm glad I can explore them with millions of strangers every morning on the radio.

How We Do What We Do

Here's a dirty little secret: I am *not* a morning person.

Messed up, right? I've spent over twenty years working the morning shift. I go live to millions of people every weekday at 6 a.m. You'd think by now I'd have come up with some kind of healthy morning routine like all the other morning-show hosts.

I love those articles about how much they get done before the sun comes up. They're always exfoliating their pores and making gratitude lists, and, I don't know, aligning their chakras. I read somewhere that Gayle King takes a bubble bath at three forty-five every morning.

Good for Gayle. But that's not me. If I'm in a bubble bath at 3:45 a.m., I'm not having an early morning—I'm having a late night.

Here's my morning routine. My alarm goes off less than an hour before my show goes live. I lurch into the shower, still half-asleep, and try to remember if I'm going to be on camera today. In other words, can I get away with a hoodie?

And then I'm stumbling through the apartment to the door, trying not to trip over Max, ignoring all the dirty dishes we were too tired to clean up before we went to bed last night.

That's it. No Pilates. No sun salutations. I'm not aligning *shit*. Who has time for that? Even though my commute takes ten minutes max, I'm already running late.

As soon as I get off the elevator, I walk into a tornado.

Actually, *walk* is probably the wrong word. It's more like *sprint*. That's what happens when you show up two minutes before you go on the air.

Sometimes people ask me how we plan out what we're going to do on the show every morning. The answer is . . . we don't. Right before showtime, we all just kind of appear in the studio. It's like the opening of *The Simpsons*: all of us suddenly bursting into the studio at the exact same moment. Except instead of piling onto a couch, we're landing in front of our microphones.

My microphone, by the way, is golden. It was a gift from the Electro-Voice company. I've been accused of acting like an asshole for using it, but hey, you'd use it, too, if they gave you a gold metallic one. BUT THEY DIDN'T.

I've worked in all kinds of studios over the years. But this is the first one with a penis table.

Yeah, *penis table*. No, there aren't penises *on* it. Usually. But even though I swear we didn't intend it this way, the big table we all sit around every morning is shaped like a big beige dick.

I'm sitting at the base of a semicircle, with a long table stretching directly out from the other side. In front of me, on the . . . well, on the balls . . . is a huge sound board. Dozens of buttons and switches and sliders and meters and clocks. I don't know what they all do—but they look important.

Even more important, of course, than the flashy gear and shiny toys are the people who make the show happen—starting with the two women sitting on the other side of the board, at the, uh, base of the shaft.

On my right is Danielle, who's already got her laptop open, scanning for today's Hollywood buzz and shopping on Amazon. I've been spending the morning with her for twenty years. I don't know what I'd do if I looked over there and didn't see her face.

Across from her is Gandhi—the newest member of the family. She's got so much energy, and such a wicked sense of humor. People are always tweeting at the show that they wish they could hang out with her because they feel like she's not just a radio host, but their friend. Hard to get a better compliment in this business.

Brody hangs out behind Gandhi. Never sits down. All morning, he'll be bouncing around on his heels, slipping us notes with joke pitches. But right now, he's probably complaining about some restaurant that didn't give him free dessert even after he posed for a picture with the owner.

We put Greg T down at the tip, right in front of the glass separating us from Scotty B (another twenty-year vet who meticulously produces our show for our mother-ship station, Z100), because where else on the big morning-show penis would you put the guy with the round, pink shaved head? Like Brody, Greg T always comes in hot—way louder than you'd think anybody could be at six in the morning.

Skeery's somewhere over my left shoulder. He never stops moving, the entire show. He's looking at four screens at once: one monitor for incoming texts from listeners, another with all the ad breaks cued up, another for playing songs and clips and sound effects, and the fourth screen? His phone. He's always on Instagram. Always. On top of Skeery's monitor rig, there's a bright white light that flashes like a police siren whenever someone's calling in on the hotline.

We all say hi to Froggy, who's joining us from Florida via a TV mounted over Greg T's shoulder, and then things get quiet for a second while we put on our headphones and test the levels on our microphones. (All of us except for Skeery, who doesn't need a microphone—when he has something to say, he practically leaps up on my shoulders and yelps it out while humping me like a horny golden retriever.)

Orbiting around us is our senior executive producer, Straight Nate. He's always running in and out of the studio, doing his frantic best to signal when we need to cut to a break or when I forget to mention a sponsor. Nate's got a tough job. He does all the stuff I don't have the patience or the brain power to do. Which is a lot.

That's a lot of people around our penis table. But you've got a whole lot more family members to meet. They're in constant motion around the studio, and it seems like every five minutes the door is swinging open and another friendly face is sprinting in.

Try to keep up, because they'll only be in here for a minute before they have to run: Garrett pops in during the eight o'clock hour to play sound clips, plus he's a nonstop prep machine. Web Girl Kathleen keeps us merged into the social media lane and is so DIY driven she can make a lamp out of a pineapple. Coaster

Boy Josh is the master magician behind our signature sound production (he's what we call our "creative director"). Jake is the mastermind of all of our video for social and web. All self-taught. Producer Sam, in addition to being the on-air spiritual center of the show, also ensures sponsors' spots are lined up and organized. Our newest addition is Diamond. Such a superstar. Always on the phone calls and texts looking for life on the outside for us to put on the show.

And then there is my lovingly abused assistant, Andrew Pugliese. He technically works for me and my company, yet he's everyone's best friend and confidant. The crap he has to put up with from me is monumental. Constant travel changes; keeping up with all personal business—basically keeping my life in order because I'm incapable of doing that. Really. Thank you, Andrew.

Point is: I might be the guy who gets to talk into a golden microphone, but around here, it's a family affair.

As for the show's actual topics, well, we mostly pull from staffers and interns, talking about what they did last night or the funny T-shirt they wore into the office this morning. We have guests ranging from Grammy Award–winning artists to celebrity chefs to heroes from local charities. But the observations and contributions from our family members are our foundation.

We could actually turn off the world and do a show with just us. And some mornings, when I look around the table, it feels like it is just us.

Every show feels like being strapped into a roller coaster. As the last few ads and promos finish, you can feel it slowly creaking upward to the top. You're holding your breath for the drop. And then the red light comes on, and the mics go live, and the roller coaster plunges down, and there's no telling what's going to happen next.

It's like cracking open that first bottle of tequila with all your friends. You don't know where the night's going to go, just that it's going to go fast.

Of course, we don't just make it up as we go along. We get notes from writers and producers every morning—packets of interesting bits pulled from news and culture outlets. *Happy birthday, Demi Lovato! Here's a viral clip of a goat that screams like a human baby! A small town in Georgia just elected a sixteen-year-old as mayor. Ooh, look, a new trailer for the next big Marvel movie! Did you know it's National Banana Split Day?*

But it's the random, unstructured moments in between where the magic really happens.

Think about it this way. If you have a job you love, odds are it's because of the people you work with. In between flipping burgers or cleaning teeth or processing TPS reports or whatever it is you actually do, there are all the inside jokes and mini-dramas you share with your coworkers that turn them into something like family.

Well, you know that old joke about how they should make the whole plane out of the indestructible black box? Imagine how much fun your life would be if all the small talk, all the gossip, all the silly arguments over whether a hot dog is a sandwich or not, turn into the most important debates in the history of the world—imagine if that stuff was your whole job. It'd be like a box of Lucky Charms that was all marshmallows.

That's what my job is like. Yes, we play songs and we do prank calls and we talk about the news and we interview guests. But the real show is the stuff in between.

Greg T is pissed because Skeery's wearing a Rutgers T-shirt even though he didn't go to Rutgers—is that a party foul or is Greg T just being, you know, Greg T about it, getting worked up over nothing? Wait, there's a caller who wants to know if she can wear a Harvard sweatshirt she stole from a guy she dated who went there? That seems acceptable, right? Call it a "screwvenir"! Suddenly, Greg T is singing the Rutgers fight song at the top of his lungs. For some reason, he and Skeery are switching shirts? Let's get Kathleen in here with her iPhone and put the video online!

Gandhi was at a bar last night and saw a guy she's sure is a famous actor, but she couldn't place the name—let's all try to figure it out. Was it Jude Law? No, this guy was way too short. Wait, how tall is Jude Law? Isn't it weird how we always imagine celebrities to be taller than they are? Someone heard a rumor that Tom Cruise is really only five foot one. That's gotta be one of those urban legends, right? Like the one about Alan Rickman and the gerbil! What? No. That's Richard Gere. Are you sure? "He's five foot ten!" yells Skeery. Huh? "Jude Law." Thanks, Skeery.

Oh my God, Danielle brought in pastries! Holy cow, did you try one of these big flaky ones with the cream inside? What are they called? Lobster tails! I tried to cook dinner last night and I totally screwed it up, so I'm hungry today. Where'd you get these, Danielle? Oh, that's right next to this diner I went to on a date once. Who brings a date to a diner? It was romantic! What's the worst place you've ever gone on a first date? Text us!

It doesn't take much to set us off. And the same is true of our listeners. Skeery's screen is full of texts: *I LOVE JUDE LAW!* and *I once went on a first date to the TGI Fridays in Penn Station* and *Greg T should calm down LOL* and *PLEASE PLAY "DESPACITO" I NEED TO DANCE OR I WILL FALL ASLEEP AT MY DESK.*

I try to keep things at least sort of on track. I have this thing in my head I call a "spectrum clock." Research tells us that the average listener is only listening in for twenty or thirty minutes at a time. And in that short time, I want them to get the whole sampler of what our four-hour show is about: a juicy piece of gossip about the Kardashians, a call from a listener riled up about her boyfriend's Internet search history, a good-news story about a military veteran with a prosthetic leg who just set a marathon record, a lively debate about whether it's okay to text during a movie (for the record: hell no).

And on top of that, I know that a lot of our listeners listen at the same time every day—say, from 7:10 to 7:35 a.m., on their ride to work. So I'm always aware that I never want the show to fall into the same predictable rhythm. I want every day's listening experience to be a little different.

It's the same with the music we play. The station has a computer program that categorizes every song by its attributes—this one's a dance track with a female singer, that one has a grunge guitar—and makes sure we don't play two straight songs with too many common features.

So yeah, there's some science to it. But there's no manual for this sort of thing. It's all being directed in my head.

By ten o'clock, I'm wiped. And my radio day is almost over. On some days, anyway.

Sometimes there are a few loose ends to address: talking about what worked today and what didn't and what's next. *That "Chef Le T" bit was hilarious—nice work, Greg. We had a screwup on the phones and two different callers got told they had won the thousand bucks—what happened there? We're doing Celebrity Jeopardy next Wednesday—Skeery, make sure the sound effects are ready.*

Meanwhile, we're all eating whatever's left from whatever got brought into the studio that day. That's one of the hallmarks of *Elvis Duran and the Morning Show*: free food. And, yes, that can be tricky for a guy who's struggled with his weight.

I never eat breakfast at home. I just assume that at some point before ten there's going to be food in the studio. Not necessarily breakfast food, mind you. Sometimes a whole tableful of cheesesteaks will just sort of materialize outside the glass. Sometimes it's pizza. Sometimes it's cupcakes. You haven't truly lived until you've eaten an entire Italian sub at seven fifteen in the morning. Breakfast of champions. We all get cranky if nothing has arrived by around halfway through the show. And we're not above putting out a call for free food over the air.

Once the meeting's over, we record a quick podcast and maybe a video or two for the website. We're not just a radio show anymore—haven't been for a long time. We have so many different ways to reach our audience—but that means we have so many different kinds of content to create.

Back in the old days of radio, the show was the whole job. "You do your four and hit the door," the saying went, and that left twenty hours in the day for sleep and exercise and getting into trouble. But these days, my afternoons and evenings are often as hectic as my mornings.

If it were up to me, when Alex got home from his job at the Staten Island Zoo, I'd already be in sweatpants, with something tasty simmering away on the stove, something stupid cued up on Netflix, and our dog Max already curled up on the couch, ready for a big night in. And every once in a while, that's exactly what I get to do.

But those nights are few and far between. And every once in a while, the party will keep rolling into the night and make it all the way back home, where, not long before Gayle King is getting up for her bubble bath, Alex and I will sack out among a graveyard of empty wineglasses.

Just another day at the office.

CHAPTER 12

An Old Dog Learns Some New Tricks

You never know when the turning points in your life are going to come. You don't get to find out in advance which days are going to be ordinary and which ones are going to wind up changing everything forever. I guess that's why my mom told me to always wear clean underwear.

I wasn't wearing *any* underwear the day I first met Steven Levine. That's because we met at a pool party. Alex and I had only been barely, sort-of dating, and we were on our first "fly-away" together. It was a listeners' weekend at the world famous Fontainebleau Miami Beach.

Anyway, on our first weekend away, I was on my best behavior. Or as close to it as I could manage. And at the pool, Alex introduced me to a friend of his, a cheerful guy named Steven. At the time, Steven was the publicist for an artist named Kat DeLuna—a great talent and a really nice person who worked her ass off and earned some real success. And when Steven found out that the host of

New York's number one Top 40 morning show was at the party, he went over to the pool club's DJ and got him to play the latest Kat DeLuna single over the sound system, just so I could hear it.

Hmm, I thought. *This guy's pushy! What an asshole! I just want to relax and don't need to be promoted.* Well, as it turns out, Steven Levine is a sweetheart of a guy. Hilarious. A little nuts.

The next time I saw Steven was at a sushi bar on Staten Island. Alex and I were there with a bunch of his friends and co-workers from the zoo, celebrating the opening of a new exhibit I'd helped raise money for. For some reason, a reporter and photographer from the *Staten Island Advance*—the local paper of record, and Staten Islanders pronounce it "AD-vance," thank you very much—showed up. Maybe they came because, for Staten Islanders, Fushimi was the place to be that year. Or maybe somebody called in a tip.

I never found out if that somebody was Steven Levine. But he was there at Fushimi. And when the photographer from the *Advance* asked our table if he could take a picture, Steven leapt into action, corralling everyone and organizing us so that I was sitting right in the middle of the shot, surrounded by everyone from the zoo. Later, he explained how he had talked to the reporter, convincing him that instead of a story about a minor local celebrity and some friends hitting the town, he should write a story about the exciting new exhibit at the zoo and how hard we had all worked to make it possible.

Hmm, I thought. *This guy's* really *good. But he's still a little pushy.*

That's when Steven and I started talking about the possibility of him coming to work for me full-time. I hadn't exactly been in the market for a publicist. As far as I was concerned, I was already famous enough. We were on top in the ratings, and we'd achieved our goal of syndicating the show across the country. I had a hot young boyfriend and enough money to take people out for sushi. I kind of felt like life could just go on like this forever and I'd be just fine.

Plus, I'm lazy. Everything Steven suggested just sounded like a lot of extra work.

But here's something I've learned: Even though you never know *when* your life is about to change forever, sometimes you can make a pretty good guess about *who* might wind up changing it. My whole career, I've gravitated toward people whose instincts I trust, whose company I enjoy, and—most important—who know a lot about stuff I know nothing about. All my friends and mentors from my career in radio fit that description: Steve Kingston, Tom Poleman, Dennis Clark. And even though I couldn't yet imagine what I wanted the next phase of my life to look like, I had the feeling that Steven Levine might be the kind of person I'd want around to help me make it happen.

It didn't take long for Steven to hatch a golden idea: It was time to take my talents to TV.

At first, I wasn't interested. Steven had told me from day one that there was value in being seen as well as heard, but I had friends who did TV, and I'd seen how much work it took to get camera-ready every day. I was much happier going to work in a ripped T-shirt and sweatpants—doing my four and hitting the door.

But then Steven explained what he had in mind. What if, he

said, we could get an artist—let's say Taylor Swift—to come into the studio for an interview, and we get her people to agree to have *Entertainment Tonight* come in that day as well. That way, while the radio show is on commercial break, you could ask Taylor a few questions for *ET*.

It was win-win-win. *Entertainment Tonight* gets an exclusive Taylor Swift interview. Taylor gets to reach two different audiences in one stop. And I get national exposure on a widely syndicated TV show. All without me having to do much more than wear clean clothes and slap on a little foundation. Uh, okay. Begrudgingly.

But, wait—there's more! What if we invited a national music magazine like *Rolling Stone* to come in, too? They could witness the whole thing and use any of the content, and maybe even ask Taylor a question or two of their own. Oooh, and let's tell the Getty Images folks, too—they can come in and snap some pictures of Taylor to put up online. We'll even create our very own *Elvis Duran and the Morning Show* step-and-repeat (that's the thing you take pictures in front of on the red carpet, with logos repeating to make sure they're in every shot)—that way, we can get our branding in those pictures.

I didn't exactly get why Steven was so excited about branding, and I still wasn't all that interested in being a TV star, but I liked the plan because it could make our show a destination for more artists. I loved doing interviews, but it was often like pulling teeth to get the big stars to come in. If we could offer them a little more value, and it got us new and better interviews, I was all in.

Right away, Steven's plan worked like a charm. All of a sudden, our studio was Grand Central Terminal for celebrities and TV crews. And it seemed like every day we figured out another way to make our arrangement more beneficial to everyone involved. At one point, we even had swag tables set up outside the studio where, for example, a jewelry line could bring in their stuff, and on the way out the door, artists would get to pick up some earrings to take home—the idea being that maybe the celeb would post a photo wearing them. Everybody wins! We went from being a sleepy little radio show with high ratings to being a loud, boisterous media generator with even higher ratings!

That said, I still wasn't entirely comfortable in front of a camera. And while I'd spent decades perfecting the art of radio, I was still a total rookie when it came to TV. One night early on, Steven came over to watch an *Access Hollywood* segment I'd filmed. I cringed when I saw myself on the screen—it was never pleasant to be reminded how overweight I was in those days. Then Steven paused the tape.

"Look," he said, pointing. "Your skin! It's so shiny! You've *got* to let me put some bronzer on you."

Okay. Next time, I let him at me with the makeup brush. He was careful and thorough, finishing with just a dab on the tip of my nose. "Boop!"

But when we gathered to watch the interview on TV, I realized that he had *way* overdone it. I looked like a New Jersey sunset. Steven knew it, too. When the segment ended, he was scared to even look at me. Instead, he carefully asked, "So how old is this TV?"

Nice try. I almost swatted him. "Steven, I look like an orange!" We laughed so hard.

And eventually, we figured out the *right* amount of bronzer. In fact, to this very day—even though he's regarded as one of the most successful and high-powered PR gurus in the business—Steven always has that bronzer brush ready to go at a moment's notice (and he always finishes with that little "boop!" on the nose). Our dear friend Bobbi Brown (as in Bobbi Brown, cosmetic and lifestyle maven) even developed our own customized "Elvis Duran" bronzer. And it's always sold out in Japan for some reason. I don't get it.

Looking back at it now, that day at the pool in Miami was a turning point in my life. Of course, I didn't realize it until much later. And it wasn't for the reason you might think.

Truth is, even to this day, the extra fame that comes with being on TV sometimes doesn't really excite me. But by bringing Steven into my life, I wound up discovering something new and exciting about a job I thought I'd mastered.

After all, I'd been doing radio for a quarter century. I could "do radio" with my eyes closed. But I really leaned into mastering the art of the interview. Actually, I'd never thought of it as an art at all. Until Steven's brainstorm, the interviews we did were infrequent and, to be honest, kind of boring. An artist would come in looking unhappy to be up so early, trailed by the manager who'd talked them into doing the show. I'd ask a couple of basic questions, plug the record, and then throw it to the single—and they'd be out the door, on to their next appointment, where they'd give the exact same answers to the exact same questions.

Rinse, repeat.

But now that our studio was becoming a destination for artists eager to get multiple bites at the publicity apple, I started paying more attention to that part of my job. If I was going to get to do all these interviews, why not try to make them worth listening to?

As I mentioned earlier, I've always been a big Howard Stern fan. Everyone in radio is. One of the things that makes Howard a genius is that he does the best interviews in the business. And the way he does it is that he knows exactly how to make his guest uncomfortable in just the right way. He puts people on the spot, and he pokes and prods at the sensitive places where they're afraid to be touched.

I'm not saying that to criticize. Howard doesn't do it to be an asshole. He does it because that's how he gets his guests to a place of honesty and openness. A Howard Stern interview might be a little edgy, maybe even awkward, but it's always must-listen radio, because you know you're going to hear stuff you won't hear in any of the ten thousand other interviews that guest has done to promote whatever it is they're promoting.

Howard's talent has brought him a long way from where he started. The book he put out earlier this year is fascinating—all about the conversations he's had with his guests over the years. Remember all that "Butt Bongo Fiesta" stuff from back in the early '90s? That's not who he is, or what the show is, anymore.

Anyway, as you can tell, I love Howard. And I wanted to be a great interviewer, too. But I knew I couldn't do it the way Howard did. That's just not who I am. And if I tried to be that guy, I'd fail miserably.

But what I figured out was that I could get to the same place via another route. Instead of forcing my guests into a place of honesty by making them squirm, I could coax it out of them by making them as *comfortable* as possible. When they walked into our studio, I wanted them to feel like they weren't going before a panel of cross-examiners, but rather meeting old friends at the bar for a drink.

These days, anyone who wants to be a big star needs media training, and most of them have gotten plenty of it by the time they blow up. The number one rule when it comes to interviews: *Only tell an interviewer what* you *want them to know*. So what good does it do anybody for me to ask Katy Perry a bunch of TMZ-style questions about who she's sleeping with or feuding with when we all know she's not going to answer? And, for that matter, who wants to hear me ask Ed Sheeran whether he hopes he wins another Grammy when we all know he's going to insist that it's an honor just to be nominated?

Instead, I started trying to ask the kinds of questions you'd ask someone on a third date. Questions with open-ended answers that would hopefully let me, and my audience, get to know the human being sitting across the table, instead of just the image they'd constructed as a vehicle for their music.

As someone who's been an introvert all my life, I've found that the best way to get comfortable around other people is to be curious about them. People like talking about themselves. And if you ask the right questions, not only will they enjoy talking to you, you'll probably learn something interesting you've never thought about before.

That doesn't just apply to celebrities, by the way. *Everyone* is interesting if you take the time to find out who they really are. That's why, when I meet new people out in the world, I always want to know about their lives. What makes them tick. Yeah, it's easier just to talk about the weather, but then you're just bouncing questions off the shell we all put up to keep our true selves hidden, and what's the point of that?

Celebrities tend to have a thicker, shinier shell than most people, but I still talk to them the same way I'd talk to you if we were sitting next to each other at an airport bar, each of us a couple drinks in. It doesn't have to be some big dramatic confessional. You can learn a lot about the world just by asking people what it was like where they grew up, or how they wound up in the line of work they're in, or where they went on their last vacation. Everybody's life is different. Everybody has something to teach you.

I'm fascinated by artists who are also songwriters. I am *so not* a songwriter. The whole thing is totally foreign to me. Every songwriter has a different process. Some write the music first and only put words to it at the end. Others walk around with a notebook full of lyrics waiting for a melody to match.

Some work alone, holing up in the woods for weeks at a time, waiting for that spark of genius that tells them they've just given birth to a big hit. Others like to collaborate with a writing partner, bouncing drafts back and forth over text.

Many of the best interviews I've done have been the ones where we dig deep into this stuff. Like when Charlie Puth—a lifelong music geek who's been playing with keyboards since he was a kid growing up on the Jersey Shore—played back one of the writing sessions he'd recorded on his iPhone, just messing around with chords, waiting for the melody to emerge. Or when Sia told us she'd never wanted to be an artist herself, just a writer, until she recorded a demo of "Titanium" to send to David Guetta, who loved it so much that he went ahead and used her voice in the final track. ("Did that piss you off?" I asked her. She laughed. "No way—I bought a house from that song!")

Other times, we'll welcome guests into the conversations we've been having with each other in the studio and with our callers. Pharrell once came in for an interview, and I was planning to ask him about his latest single, but we'd spent the previous segment talking about sexism, and he'd been listening from the green room. So he wound up telling us about the women in his own life, and how important they'd been to him, and pretty soon we were all reflecting on the way women are treated in our society and what each of us can do to change things. Nobody had planned for our interview to go in that direction—Pharrell least of all—but he was so thoughtful. He had the whole room in tears.

"I don't know how you got that out of me," he said afterward. Neither did I. But, just like with any conversation, you sometimes know when you've hit a rich vein. So you just stick with it and let it come naturally.

Yeah, we might start the interview asking about the new album. But because we just let the conversation flow, we wind up in places nobody expects.

Like the time we had Meghan Trainor on and wound up talking about meditation. She'd struggled with anxiety, and told us about the app she'd used to find peace—it's called Calm (free plug). People are sometimes resistant to trying meditation because they think they'll suck at it, but, as we talked about, you don't get a grade on how well you do it. As Meghan put it, "Just taking the time to know that you did that, that you were silent for that long, is really cool." Then we started talking about a book I love by a friend of mine, Dan Harris—it's called *10% Happier* (another free plug). I don't know if anyone listened in hoping to get tips on finding inner peace, but I'm pretty sure it was more useful to the audience than the usual celebrity interview.

Or the time we had Mike Posner on and wound up talking about parents. His father had just passed away, and he told us how the last moments he spent with him had helped to inspire some of the emotions on his new album. So I told him about how, as my dad was winding down, I apologized for this whole list of things I imagined my parents must have been mad about—like how I was an awful student and wasted their hard-earned money on tuition, or the time when I was a kid and took the family car out for a joyride and almost got arrested. Turned out they hadn't held a grudge. And I just wish I hadn't waited to find that out.

That really connected with Mike. "I used to think my mom was such a burden when I was a teenager," he said. "Then something clicked at, like, twenty-three, twenty-four, I wish it was earlier, and it was like, *You are so lucky you have a mom that close right now.* To have someone that loved you before you even remember—it's just a gift you can never pay back."

Or the time we had rising-star singer Donna Missal on and wound up talking about confidence. Like a lot of artists, Donna had to support her music by working as a bartender—but unlike most of them, she never really told anyone at her "day job" about her real passion. Why not? I asked.

"I was embarrassed," she said. "I was scared that if I tried and I failed that's all I would be—just a failure. I didn't want anybody to know. I don't think that I had the confidence yet to back myself up. And it took many years to get there."

That got us off on a discussion about how to develop that kind of confidence. I knew there were people listening who were in the exact same place on their own journeys, struggling to find the will to take a risk. For Donna, it was constant work and positive affirmation—and giving herself the patience to develop her career slowly.

These are all conversations we could have had with anyone, even if they weren't famous pop stars. These are conversations we all have with each other in our own lives every day. And in a way, that's the whole idea.

I think treating artists like human beings instead of commodities is a way of showing respect to them, but it's also a way of showing respect to our listeners. Sometimes we think of pop stars as if they're a different species—like they breathe through gills or something. But we work to connect them with their fans on a deeper level, because I always feel like we should *all* feel connected, all the time—connected by the things that make us interesting, and vulnerable . . . and human!

One of my favorite artists of the past few years is Logic. His whole life goes into every line of every song. He is always telling you *his* story. And the lessons you get from his music—be honest, do right by people, don't be afraid to be yourself—are the ones he's learned the hard way.

When we had Logic on the show, Danielle's fourteen-year-old nephew, Vincent, got to take the day off of school to come in and meet him. And it was cool to watch this quiet, shy kid get to meet his absolute favorite artist. What was even better, though, was that Logic got him to open up in a way his family rarely witnessed. We actually let Vincent do part of the interview, and listening to them talk about Logic's lyrics and how they'd helped Vincent through tough times, it didn't feel like watching an artist and a fan. It felt like watching two people share something real.

And isn't that why we all love art? Painters and musicians and actors—they don't feel different emotions than we do. Their genius comes from the fact that they're able to take those universal emotions and create something from them that speaks to *all* of us, that helps us process our *own* feelings.

Am I getting too deep here? Should I have put down the bong a couple pages ago? All I'm saying is, for me, a good interview isn't about making someone look bad *or* good. It's about being curious, and looking for connections, and giving people space to be thoughtful about their place in the world. That's what our show is all about. And when we welcome a celebrity into our world, we invite them to share that mind-set.

Of course, sometimes, it just doesn't work. A guest will show up hungover, or upset about something, or maybe they took the red-eye from LA and they're just too exhausted to be thoughtful. I'll be honest: I don't have a lot of patience for that. To me, if you're not feeling up for giving a good interview, just stay home! We've got plenty of stuff to talk about. Come back another time.

I know that when I say that, you're imagining stars acting like divas. That *does* happen sometimes. Taio Cruz once came in wearing sunglasses and refused to take them off. He just sat there, not really answering questions, looking miserable. I was frustrated. I could tell that no matter how much energy *I* put into the interview, it was going to suck. *Why did you even bother coming in?*

Then there was the time Katy Perry showed up late, leaving us hanging. When a producer popped in to let us know her car had finally arrived, I told him to tell Katy to not bother coming up. The allotted segment time was gone and there was no way to fit her in. (To her credit, she understood, and the next day she came by to make up the interview, apologetic and, even better, *on time*—and instantly redeemed herself in our eyes.)

The same thing happened with Nicki Minaj. We were really excited to book her, and we'd even arranged for a jewelry company to set up a promotional table full of stuff so she could leave with a memorable gift. And then she didn't show up. We were so disappointed, and I was ready to write her off forever. But word got back to us that she was sorry—she'd been listening to the show in the car and had felt awful hearing us talk about how sad we were that she wasn't going to make it—and we decided to give her another chance.

It turned out to be a great interview, the first of many. Nicki is so fun. We love pushing each other's buttons. We even presented her with a diamond watch—so now she would have no excuse for not showing up on time.

That summer, on my birthday, we got a note in the studio from Nicki's assistant: *There's a black BMW downstairs with a gift for Elvis in it.* Steven ran down to meet the driver. And sure enough, when he opened the trunk, there was an insanely expensive Louis Vuitton suitcase with a note from Nicki: *Happy birthday to the king.*

*　　*　　*

Sometimes, interviews go bad and it's not really anybody's fault. Take what happened with Usher—one of those awkward stories people always bring up when they ask about celebrities I didn't click with.

I *love* Usher. Love his music. And the worst interview I ever did with him was right before the release of what, ironically, would wind up being my favorite of his albums.

Maybe he wasn't at his best to begin with that day—it was early, and he rolled into the studio not making eye contact with anyone. Seeing that he wasn't exactly thrilled to be there, I started by telling him how much I liked the first single off the album. Which was true! Every time I listened to the song, it made me feel so . . . *good*. It was, I told him, kind of like listening to a great Michael Jackson song that way.

That's when his head snapped up. "I'm not Michael Jackson," he muttered. I hadn't meant to suggest that he was! But nothing I tried would get the interview back on track. Every answer he gave was short, clipped, like he was mad at me. I glanced over at the screen where texts from the audience come in. People were pissed. "What's his problem?" "Get him off the air!" "What's wrong with this guy?"

We still had a few minutes left to go before the scheduled commercial break, but he wasn't having fun and neither was I—and, most important, neither was the audience. So, as politely as I could, I thanked him for coming in—and we cut the interview short. We didn't even take pictures for the website.

It was bad radio. But I don't think of it as a story about Usher being a jerk. To me, it was like a bad first date. You got stuck in traffic on the way there, so you're kind of flustered . . . and your phone keeps buzzing with work texts, so you're distracted . . . and the restaurant is too loud, so you have to keep repeating yourself . . . and the guy kind of looks like a bad ex from college, so you're thinking about *that* asshole . . . and it takes forever for the food to arrive, so you're hangry. . . . It's nobody's fault, but you two aren't going to be ordering dessert, let alone going back to your apartment. That's how most bad interviews happen.

Another misfire was Andy Cohen. You would *think* he and I would get along great. We're both hosts. We both love pop culture. We're both members in good standing of the Cool Gay Club. I'd read his book, and not only did I love it, I recognized a bit of myself in his story. He was a big TV fan growing up, and he talked about it like it was his babysitter. It sounded just like my experience with radio when I was alone on my grandmother's couch. We even loved a lot of the same shows.

Maybe that was the mistake I made—assuming that he and I were alike and that we would both see the interview the same way. I'd heard him on other shows: fun, lively, sassy. I thought it would be a slam dunk. But when he walked in, he was quieter than I expected. He spent a lot of time looking at his phone. And I probably should have realized that I needed to call an audible. But instead, I started the interview with what I stupidly thought would be a fun icebreaker: "So, Andy: Everyone wants to know— are you a top or a bottom?"

He didn't laugh. "Why is that important?" he asked. And the interview was doomed.

Again, I didn't take it personally. I've run into Andy a couple times at events, and he's been every bit as delightful and funny as I'd imagined. We just didn't click that day. Come to think of it, the same thing happened when we had Anderson Cooper on the show. Am I *not* a member in good standing of the Cool Gay Club? Are you guys having meetings I'm not invited to?!?!

But for the most part, I have fun doing interviews, even if they don't go exactly as planned. I've always been a big Madonna fan—talk about someone who's always known exactly who she is and refused to stray from it—but I've never had a good Madonna interview. For whatever reason, I can never seem to get her to give a straight answer. Hers is a tough shell to crack.

Then there's Mariah—my favorite diva. If you asked me: "Think fast. Who do you want to interview right this minute?" MARIAH!

She always brings drama. The fun kind. One time she came in wearing lingerie and insisted on having a fan blowing her hair dramatically throughout the whole interview, even though nobody was rolling video that day. Another time we got into a slight skirmish on the air because I started talking about how long we'd known each other and she didn't want me talking about her age. Mariah's an adventure, but she's never boring. Her performance at last year's iHeartRadio Music Festival in Las Vegas was beyond amazing. We toasted her during the backstage national interview (she supplied the wine, dahling). And during a private moment, I looked her in the eye and told her how I believed she was better than ever that night. Solid show. Fabulous interview. I went to bed that night smiling, knowing I shared the night with one of my all-time favorite superstars. And she was back on top of the world.

Some of the celebrities who famously get "knocked around" by the press—tabloid mainstays like Miley Cyrus and Justin Bieber—are among my favorite interviews. We manage to get deep with them, contrary to the image people have of them as shallow party animals. Miley always jokes that our show feels like a therapy session. But I'd rather be a therapist than a prosecutor. I also love how she refers to me as her "second-favorite gay uncle." Yes, there is a first. And I'm jealous as hell.

I almost teared up when Lady Gaga told us excitedly about how she'd grown up listening to our show, and how thrilled she was to finally be on it. She almost fainted when she heard Danielle's voice come out of her lips. Gaga is a huge fan of Danielle. But so am I!

Not surprisingly, she's a great interview. Once, we'd been talking for, I don't know, ten or fifteen minutes, and I could see out of the corner of my eye that her team was getting anxious to wrap things up so she could move on to the next thing. I think Gaga could sense it, too. And so I decided to just say what was on my mind.

"My problem with these interviews," I said, "is sometimes I wish we could just go hide in the basement, away from all these people, and keep talking."

Gaga looked surprised. "Wanna go to my basement?"

"Yeah."

"Okay," she said, without hesitation. "Well, let's go!"

"I'm not saying you need to turn on the waterworks," I said. "I just wish we had more time with you, in a different forum."

Gaga totally got what I was driving at. So we started talking about what it was like to be an artist in a world where there were so many demands on an artist's time and attention. And Gaga said something that has stuck with me ever since.

Somebody gives me a canvas at the beginning of every album cycle. And it's blank. And I'm left with a paintbrush. And I sit by myself. And that is the thing I want people to know and recognize—not just about me, but about them- selves.

You will not be defined by the people that hire you. You will not be defined by the corporate world around you. You will be defined by the ideas that are in your own heart and your own mind. And it's just you, and that brush, and that fucking canvas. And you will work hard enough that one day, you will sign only your name at the bottom of that blank page.

What's silly is, the interview wound up going viral because of something she said later on, when she started talking about the pressures of being creative and how they led her to develop a problem with marijuana. I guess that's what gets people's attention.

But if you were listening to that other part, you felt like you really *knew* this woman, and knew what went into her art. It felt like she had reached out through the radio and looked each lis- tener in the eye. She was so in touch with herself, and so willing to let her guard down. It blew me away. Even if we had to bleep the f-word.

*   *   *

Our interviews have made a lot of news over the years. Not always for the right reasons.

The day after a terrorist bombing at an Ariana Grande show in England, Katy Perry came on, and she said something I thought was really profound: "I think the greatest thing we can do is just unite and love on each other. And, like, no barriers, no borders—we all just need to coexist."

She was talking about the bullshit that goes on in the world of pop music—something she knows plenty about from the silly feud between her and Taylor Swift (or, more accurately, between her fans and Taylor's). She wasn't talking about "borders," as in the one between the US and Mexico, and she wasn't talking about "barriers" because she didn't think there should be security checkpoints at concerts. She was just talking about fighting hate with love.

But, of course, it blew up on the political blogs, with headlines like "Singer Katy Perry's Solution to Terrorism: 'No Barriers, No Borders.'" Someone even posted pictures of her house in California, pointing to the gate at her driveway and calling her a hypocrite.

Sigh.

More often, though, our show has been a place where artists come to make *good* news. They announce new albums or tours. They talk about getting engaged. They share music they've been working on and are really proud of.

Most of all, they tell stories. And the best ones are the stories about where *they* began. The stories that made our favorite artists who they are. What's crazy is, we've been doing this long enough that sometimes *we're* part of those stories.

One of the artists we've had on a lot is Halsey. She grew up in New Jersey, listening to our show—the very first time we had her on, she even told us about trying to win Jingle Ball tickets. Apparently, she'd faked sick to stay home from school so she could call in over and over again, trying to get through on the phone line she had in her bedroom. Then her mom came home early from work—just as she *finally* got through to our producer. So her mom walked in to hear her screaming. With joy! But her mom didn't know that. So she picked up the extension. Halsey told us she panicked and hung up—and only then realized she'd blown her shot at tickets.

"This station," she told us, "has been the soundtrack to my life. I mean, driving to prom, getting my license, driving to bad things—the hospital, funerals. Going to visit my grandmother. Going to visit my friends. This is the station. And the fact that I get to be the soundtrack of someone else's life now—pinch me."

No—pinch *me*.

We've had her on a bunch of times since, talking with her about everything: getting high, peeing backstage before shows, the process of putting together an album, struggling to develop your identity as an artist. It's always a great show.

Part of that is because she's such an open person. If you want to know who Halsey is, put on one of her albums. Her real self comes through in every song.

But I like to think it's also partly because she knows our show is a place where she can be herself. And I think a lot of artists have come to see our show as a place they can go to feel comfortable. To connect with their fans on a deeper level. To work through tough times. To celebrate who they really are.

Think about it. So many of these artists get asked the same questions everywhere they go. They're like champagne bottles ready to pop—all they need is to be asked the question that loosens the cork.

Knowing how to ask that question is what made our show the place artists wanted to come—and me the person they wanted to talk to. I was becoming more than just a radio host—I was someone whom both listeners and artists trusted, and that opened up lots of opportunities, not just for our radio show, but off the air, too.

It was a blast. I remember, a few years ago, emceeing a record-release party for Coldplay at the iHeartRadio Theater in Burbank, California. Chris Martin is one of my favorite artists. Even though we're not close friends, I feel like he's always so warm and welcoming, and I love how colorful and uplifting Coldplay's live performances always are. After they performed, he chased me down the hall to put a LOVE lapel pin in my shirt. "Here. Because I love you." Wow. He made me FEEL loved. It was a great show, but I didn't get to stick around for the after-party—it was straight to Van Nuys Airport to board the iHeartRadio jet for a flight back to New York, because I had to emcee *another* iHeartRadio record-release party.

This time, it was Adele, at Joe's Pub—the first place she ever performed in New York. I was still jet-lagged when I got backstage, and when we heard her sound-checking "Hello," I felt like I was dreaming.

That was another great show. She's so funny and honest. (And profane! I had to warn her to get all her four-letter words out of her system before she went on, so the bleepers back at iHeart-Radio headquarters wouldn't have to work too hard.) All I had to do was light the fuse and let her go, telling stories about growing up and writing songs and her love for her son. Adele gave us more than music that night. She gave us EVERYTHING!

It was supposed to be a private show for fans (and iHeartRadio big shots). But Steven, sneaky little devil that he is, snuck a couple of press people in—one from *Entertainment Weekly*, one from *Billboard*. The stories that came out of it were great. Although I think Steven wound up with some explaining to do.

Synergy, I guess they call it. Sometimes I'd be backstage at an event, and I'd interview the same artist for three different programs, switching out the microphone between each one. It seemed like every day Steven's hard work was opening up more opportunities.

And then, one day, he asked me, "What would you think about doing the *Today* show?"

Um, what? As in THE NBC Today *show?*

It made sense. I was becoming the go-to guy for interviews with music artists. *Today* wanted to reach out to music-loving viewers, especially in their fourth hour, hosted by Hoda and Kathie Lee. Steven kept bugging the show's producers, making the case that I would be the perfect guy for a segment introducing viewers to hot new artists. He even brought them cupcakes. And, eventually, he wore them down. I was in.

Going backstage can be kind of boring and anticlimactic. But not when it comes to the *Today* show.

When you walk into 30 Rock, there's something about that building.

Maybe it's the history of the place. NBC has been around since the beginning of time. Even before there was TV, there was NBC's radio network, housed in the same building. And back when I was fourteen years old, reading livestock reports at KMMK in McKinney before throwing it to the national feed in New York, *this very building* was where Rocky Martini was broadcasting from. I can always hear his voice echoing through the hallways. And even though it's been a long time since they used the old cathode-ray tubes to broadcast television, I always swear I can smell the dust scorching off the tubes as they heat up.

Or maybe it's the people. When we walk in, there's the familiar hubbub of makeup artists and lighting technicians and stagehands, but the folks at 30 Rock are the cream of the crop. Many of them have been around forever, like Smokey, the guy who operates the smoke machine whenever a show produced in the building calls for one. Yes, there's a guy in charge of the NBC smoke machine. And yes, I call him Smokey.

Whatever it is, even to this day—and I must have done hundreds of different Artist of the Month segments by now—every time I walk into that building, I get goose bumps.

Live TV is a whole different animal than recording a segment. It moves unbelievably fast. At first, they only gave us forty-five seconds for our segment—I'd be introduced, I'd say a couple lines about the band, the camera would pan to the singer, and they would race through their single. Or at least part of it—the show would usually cut to break somewhere after the first chorus.

Over time, though, we've been able to carve out a little more room. Now I get to actually spend a couple of minutes—an eternity in live TV!—talking with the artists about where they come from and what's inspired them.

I've even had the chance to cohost that fourth hour alongside Hoda and twice with Kathie Lee. Although I have no idea why they let me do it. Once, during a segment about dating, I slipped up and talked about how sometimes guys can be real "d-bags." Nobody in the studio said anything, but on the commercial break, someone came sprinting down from the network offices upstairs.

"Hi, Elvis," she said. "They've asked me to ask you not to use that word."

"What word?"

"Um. 'D-bags.'"

"Wait a minute," Kathie Lee piped up. "He didn't say 'douche-bags.' What if he meant 'dirtbags'?"

"Either way," said the messenger from upstairs. "We'd like you to not say it anymore."

Duly noted! Haven't said it since. At least not on TV. I guess I'll have to wait until I have my own show.

CHAPTER 13

Backstage Sucks!

You ever hear that old expression *Do what you love, and you'll never work a day in your life?*

Bullshit.

Let's say your job was to sit in a massage chair all day eating chocolate ice cream. Pretty great, right? But you'd still have to set your alarm in the morning and deal with the traffic on the way in. You'd still have a guy in the next massage chair over who eats his ice cream way too loudly and always wants to tell you about his fantasy football team. You'd still have a boss who gives you grief when you take a sick day because your stomach hurts from eating too much ice cream.

My point is, even if you love the work you do . . . it's still *work*. There's no job out there so great that, at the end of the day, it isn't still a fucking *job*.

I think about that every time I go backstage at a concert. I love concerts. It doesn't even matter who's playing. When you're singing along to the chorus with twenty thousand of your fellow fans, and the band is up there looking bigger than life, and it feels like the whole arena is about to blast off into orbit . . . I mean, is there anything better?

And not only do I go to a lot of concerts as part of my job, I get to go *backstage*. That magical place where the real party happens. Big, fancy suites with white leather couches. Bottles of expensive champagne popping like firecrackers. Glamorous people doing glamorous things. Best seat in the house, right? You'd think it would be my favorite part of my job.

Wrong. Backstage *sucks*.

First of all, it's ugly. Dark, crowded corridors. Concrete floors. Exposed pipes. It's not part of the show, so why would anyone bother to dress it up? Backstage looks like a giant auto-repair shop, or a supermarket warehouse, or an airplane hangar.

Yeah, sometimes you'll see a bottle of champagne chilling in an ice bucket. But the people drinking it aren't the ones you came to see. I mean, if you want to do shots with Rihanna's publicist's cousin who lives in town and got a backstage pass, now's your chance. But the artists themselves? Mostly they're drinking tea with honey. Maybe a 5-Hour Energy shot if they really want to get wild. I don't even smell weed in most dressing rooms anymore (although, to be fair, that might be because people seem to be more into edibles these days). For every artist who's getting turnt before going onstage, there are ten who have a very specific and disappointingly wholesome prep routine.

And sure, once in a while backstage is your chance to catch an unguarded glimpse of someone famous. You might see a backup dancer walking to the bathroom, staring at his phone. You might even get to see the back of Cardi B's head for one and a half seconds. But I promise you are not going to be hanging out with your favorite artist. There's a bunch of huge guys whose whole job is making sure nobody bothers them—in fact, when artists emerge from their dressing rooms, security usually clears the entire corridor. It's nothing personal. It's just that this is the only private time these artists are going to have to get their heads in the game before showtime. They're sitting around in sweatpants looking at Twitter. They're popping pimples and taking poops. They're complaining about the traffic on the way in from the airport or the fact that they have to get up early the next morning to do the fucking Elvis Duran show. They're not wandering around looking to make new friends.

So who *will* you see backstage? A handful of other people who got backstage passes and don't really know what to do with themselves: friends of friends, executives from the record company, other assorted hangers-on. They're the ones who are standing around, looking awkward.

But the vast majority of the people you'll encounter backstage are guys with big forearms lugging around stage lights and speakers and cases of bottled water. Venue staff muttering to each other about whether they're going to get overtime if the show runs past eleven thirty. Stage techs grabbing a snack before they have to go test the smoke machines.

In other words: people doing their jobs.

See, concerts are like reverse mullets. The party's out front. In back, it's all business. So even if you got shitty seats, and you had to pay nine bucks for a beer, and the guy sitting next to you keeps dancing on your feet during every song, you're having a better time out in the crowd than I'm having backstage. After all, you're there to party, and—like everyone else backstage—I'm there to work.

I can tell you're not convinced. Nobody ever is. That's why people are always bugging me for backstage passes. So, you know what? I'll just *show* you what backstage is really like—at our biggest concert of the whole year.

Jingle Ball started back in the 1990s. It was just a fun way to celebrate the end of the year with our fans and our favorite artists. It was kind of a mess. I remember watching Billy Idol guzzling champagne all day and then getting sick all over the place. Ah, memories.

So we kept doing the show every year, and it kept getting bigger and bigger. We moved from an arena in New Jersey to the Roseland Ballroom in Manhattan, and ultimately to the most famous venue on Planet Earth: Madison Square Garden.

Then, in 2011, we got a new CEO, Bob Pittman, who, as I mentioned before, had run MTV and AOL and had a big-time vision for the company. Clear Channel had always made its money owning radio stations and—if you can believe it—billboards, but Bob saw where the industry was heading and decided that the company (which changed its name to iHeartMedia) should get into the live event business, too.

So we launched the iHeartRadio Music Festival in Las Vegas. That was a *blast*. We didn't have any idea what we were doing running a big-time live event, and we hadn't yet hired people who did. But we figured it out. A promo director from our Miami station would volunteer to come to Vegas for the weekend to wrangle talent, and the engineers who ran the boards at Z100 helped get the sound set up, and we all got drunk and had a blast. We felt like a bunch of hillbillies puttin' on a travelin' show!

Not only did it unify our company, it made money. So we created the iHeartRadio Music Awards—another excuse to put on a big show. And we grew Jingle Ball from a fun little event at the end of the year into a national touring behemoth.

But the New York show at Madison Square Garden is still the highlight—not just the highlight of the tour, but of our whole year. It's our Super Bowl.

But the bigger Jingle Ball gets, the more work there is to do. And because the show always sells out instantly, my phone has been blowing up constantly, with calls and texts from everybody I've ever met who's looking for free tickets we don't have. Two nights ago, I was down in Philadelphia for Q102's Jingle Ball. Last night, I was at 30 Rock taping an appearance on *The Tonight Show* with Jimmy Fallon. And, of course, we did a four-hour radio show this morning.

Still, by the time I get to Madison Square Garden for tonight's show, I have to be FABULOUS! And I have a long night of work ahead of me. You're welcome to tag along backstage. But do your best to keep up, okay?

My glamorous Jingle Ball night starts with me standing at the corner of Thirty-Fourth Street and Eighth Avenue in Manhattan, freezing my fucking nipples off.

See, Dmitriy dropped me off right at what I *thought* was the

VIP entrance. And yes, Dmitriy is my driver. I have a driver. Deal with it. He's actually now a part of the family.

Dmitriy's a real character, by the way. He comes from Russia via Argentina—which, right there, is something you only say about interesting people. He *looks* like a hit man, with a shaved head and a leather jacket and a dangerous-sounding accent. But he's a teddy bear. And he's a master behind the wheel: You can tell him any two end points in the city and he'll tell you exactly how long it'll take to get from one to the other at any given time of day.

Anyway, because I got my own chauffeured ride uptown (anything north of Greenwich Village is "uptown" for me), I didn't bring an overcoat, so the only protection I have against the wind is a Dsquared2 blazer with sparkly patches of green and gray and black—call it "glamoflage."

Which would be fine, except this *isn't* the VIP entrance after all. So I start sprinting back and forth, looking for the right gate, trying to be polite to all the fun listeners I need to say hi to. Everyone seems to know who I am, but the security guards aren't impressed.

They're not jerks about it or anything. I love those guys. We've been doing the show here for so long that every time we come back it's like seeing old friends. But their list is their list, and if I'm not on it, I'm not getting past 'em.

Security guys are pretty hard-core. I remember one time in Los Angeles, we were doing the iHeartRadio Music Awards, and I was supposed to interview Madonna for a live broadcast. But I was running late, because I'd been onstage to present an award, and by the time I got backstage, Madonna's security team had kicked everybody out of her room—including the iHeartRadio people who were setting up the equipment for the interview.

I got to the door, out of breath, and a big dude told me, "You can't come in. We've got Madonna in there."

"I know!" I panted. "I'm supposed to be in there interviewing her."

He stared me up and down. "Okay," he said. "But those two"—he pointed at Alex and our friend who was tagging along—"they gotta stay out."

This guy was bigger than the three of us put together, but I held my ground. "We're all coming in." You gotta defend your territory.

The interview turned out fine. But I could tell that big dude was just waiting for me to mess up once so he would have a reason to kick my ass.

Finally, I find the entrance where my name *is* on the list, and I make it inside through the metal detector. I see my publicist, Steven, who's texting furiously, and my assistant, Andrew, who looks like he hasn't slept in weeks. Andrew hands me a fistful of passes: a green one marked PRODUCTION that gets me up onstage, a black one marked GIFT LOUNGE, and a red-and-blue one for the open bar (although it'll be hours before I can finally make it in there).

But what Andrew *doesn't* have is a map, and we soon find ourselves lost in the bowels of Madison Square Garden, like that scene in *This Is Spinal Tap* where the band can't find its way onto the stage. Every hallway we turn down looks exactly the same: fluorescent lighting, low ceilings, the occasional New York Rangers poster. We try to get on an elevator, but it's jammed full of guys in suits who don't seem to know or care that I'm the emcee of the show they bought expensive tickets to see. So we take the stairs, but the "back way" Andrew knows about turns out to be another dead end.

At one point, we fling open what we think is the door to the arena, only to find . . . a boxing ring?!?! Apparently the Jingle Ball isn't the only show at MSG tonight, because there's a whole other arena set up for what I later find out is a lightweight unification bout. For about half a second, I wonder if I should just take the hint from the universe, give up on trying to find my way to backstage, abandon the radio business, and start my boxing career—but I probably can't fight in this jacket anyway.

Eventually we find the right elevator. And soon we're walking past the loading dock, where roadies are hauling in the last of the heavy black cases that hold all the instruments and amplifiers and other stuff you need to put on a big-time concert. All these cases are just stacked up in this big, open, warehouse-looking space, like some kind of rock-and-roll Stonehenge. But watch out: These guys have been unloading all day, and they're going to be here long after the fans leave packing everything back up, and they're in no mood to wait for you to get out of their way.

That's another thing about backstage: You have to keep your head on a swivel. Zone out for even half a second, and you could trip over a wire as thick as your forearm. Or crash into a production assistant in a headset sprinting to deliver updated specs to the lighting booth. Or get swept up in a mob of fans being ushered to a meet-and-greet. Or get run right the fuck over by a caterer pushing a trolley full of hummus. And no, you can't have any. That's Khalid's hummus. That's why it's covered in plastic wrap.

I'm on my way to the aforementioned "Gift Lounge," but it's taking forever. Every five feet, someone shouts my name. I'm constantly stopping to take pictures with listeners (remembering to tuck my credentials inside my jacket, because who wants *those* in your selfie?), or say hi to industry friends I haven't seen since last year's Jingle Ball. At one point, Santa walks right past me, and I turn to say hi, but I almost get mowed down by the camera crew following him for some kind of taped piece.

And when I finally make it through the gauntlet to the Gift Lounge, the name turns out to be kind of an overstatement. No, they're not giving away Rolexes. And it's not even a lounge at all. It's just a section of this big-ass warehouse floor that they've curtained off and filled with a dozen or so booths where our favorite media partners are giving away free stuff to the celebrities in hopes that they will post about it on social media.

Aha, you're saying, *here comes the cool part: free stuff!* And yeah, when Uncle Johnny comes to Jingle Ball, he practically brings a shopping cart so he can pack it full of swag. But I don't have time to fill my pockets. I've got work to do.

In the very back of the heavily guarded swag lounge, I'm headed for what they want me to call the "Mercedes-Benz Interview Lounge." In reality, it's just the back corner of this makeshift "room," where there's a tiny little stage illuminated by bright white stage lights. Welcome to my glamorous backstage headquarters. They don't even give me a dressing room.

There are already two dozen iHeart staffers crammed into this little space. They're setting up cameras, printing out little cards with the stuff I need to know, texting with talent wranglers to make sure everybody's on the same page. All I want is a cocktail and maybe a lint brush, but instead Steven just thrusts my schedule into my hands: interview, interview, interview, quick onstage appearance, interview, interview, interview, introduce artist, interview, interview, introduce artist, interview. . . . The good news tonight: All the artists I'm interviewing are friends, and I actually love seeing them. Especially tonight—hours after most of them have been announced as Grammy nominees. So there's a festive feeling in the air.

But notice what's *not* on my itinerary. No "enjoy the show." No "hit up the open bar." I don't even know when I'm supposed to find time to pee. And even as I'm trying to wrap my mind around everything I need to remember tonight, Steven's on the phone trying to cram even more interviews into the schedule. Will Cardi B let us come see her in her dressing room? Does Khalid have five minutes for a quick pop-by? There's a listener here who led a very successful campaign on Twitter hoping to meet Shawn Mendes—can we make that happen?

Right now, though, I'm getting kicked out of the Mercedes-Benz Interview Lounge so that my buddy Maxwell can interview a South Korean boy band called Monsta X. I can only imagine what the terrifyingly young guys in this band are thinking right now. And I'd love to stay and watch—especially because they're all wearing leather—but this could be my only chance tonight to do the one thing I try to do for myself at every show.

So I slip under the curtain, flash my green PRODUCTION badge a couple times, and all of a sudden, I'm standing on the floor of Madison Square Garden.

As chaotic as it is backstage, the arena itself is eerily quiet. The show is sold out—we're gonna have twenty thousand people going nuts in here tonight—but the doors won't open for another hour. And while there are a few people wandering around, using the empty room for meetings, I've pretty much got the floor to myself.

I take a moment to look up at the stage. You wouldn't know it, because it's made to look effortless, but there is some serious engineering going on up there. The stage itself is a big turntable, and it rotates after every set. While one act is performing, the next one is setting up behind the curtain. When we first started doing Jingle Ball, we had to wait twenty or thirty minutes between acts. Not anymore. We've become a well-oiled, spinning machine.

Then I turn around and look out at the sea of empty seats. Each one is about to be filled with someone who's been looking forward to tonight since the moment they got their ticket. I know it might be a little corny, but taking that moment always reminds me to stay focused on what all this work is *for*. All year long, we try to help our audience connect with the artists they love. And tonight is a way to make that connection truly special. Someone out there is going to have had a shitty day, or a shitty year, and we're going to have a chance to lift them out of it. Someone out there is going to take a picture they'll look at over and over again.

And more than one someone out there is going to be dreaming about getting up on that stage someday. I'll never forget the first year Lady Gaga played the Jingle Ball. She walked out on the stage at the sold-out Garden and pointed to the seat where she'd sat the first time she came to one as a young fan. Apparently she'd gotten to meet me that night, and had told me that she couldn't wait until I was playing *her* songs on our show and introducing *her* on our stage. Goose bumps. I wonder who'll be sitting in that seat tonight.

I'm not going to have the chance to be out here with everyone, experiencing that rush, so I take a mental picture in advance to inspire myself to put all my energy into my tiny little part of the show.

And then it's back to work.

My first interview of the night is with Sabrina Carpenter. One of my favorites. She's doing eight of our Jingle Balls this year, which is insane, but that's the kind of work ethic she's always had. I first got to know Sabrina when she was just seventeen, although she has an old soul—and, by the time I was introducing her as my Artist of the Month on the *Today* show, she had already released her second album. In addition to starring in a TV show.

Now she's nineteen, which is still ridiculously young, but she's put out yet *another* great record, and when she sweeps into the room in a long, flowy dress that looks like a disco ball, she's confident and funny and looks like a star. I'm excited to see her (and her mom, who's in the mob of people following her around like a swarm of bees). This is the best part of the whole night—catching up with old friends I don't get to see enough of. But I only have two minutes with her—barely enough time to congratulate her on her big year—and it happens under these glaring spotlights, with dozens of people buzzing around, and we're standing at that weird TV angle where we're not quite facing each other, and

I have to remember to say "Mercedes-Benz Interview Lounge" at least once.

And I know Sabrina's excited to see me, too, but she has a million other things to do tonight, and this is just one of them. Plus, this is her first time playing the Garden, and even though she doesn't *look* nervous, how could she *not* be? Either way, we're barely finished saying hello when it's time to say goodbye, and then she's off to whatever's next, and so am I.

By now, business is picking up in the Gift Lounge. Pauly D from *Jersey Shore* just walked in with the Bella Twins from WWE. There's a hot rumor circulating that somebody heard Shawn Mendes doing vocal warm-ups in a bathroom, and some fans are trying to figure out which bathroom it might be. Alex is here along with his uncles Anthony and Joel and his aunt Janet—they're already partying hard. Steven ducks in to freshen up my bronzer. And, thank GOD, Andrew brings me a Tito's and water.

Over the course of the next few hours, I hit my stride as I do interview after interview after interview. Bebe Rexha tells me about getting nominated for the Best New Artist Grammy that very morning—"My body just completely shut down!" she giggles. Shawn Mendes (a Grammy nominee as well) gets a huge cheer when he walks in, and, yes, we get that Twitter fan her picture with him. Meghan Trainor shows up trailed by her fiancé and a stylist in a bright green peacoat whose whole job appears to be making sure Meghan's pink hair is properly tucked behind her ear. Dua Lipa floats in wearing an amazing blue dress—a *different* amazing dress than the one she's about to perform in.

The room is crowded, and it's hot, and I can barely hear myself think. And the only break I get is when it's time for me to hit the stage.

The rest of the crew is already huddled underneath the rickety stairs that lead up to the stage itself, looking over our little script. It's just a quick hello to the crowd, but it's Madison Square fucking Garden, and walking out there is going to be a thrill. We're not nervous, exactly, but I can tell everyone's got a lot of adrenaline. Gandhi's cracking jokes about going out there and doing some X-rated material, and I'm *pretty* sure she's kidding. Danielle looks fabulous, with her hair done up for the night. Brody's buzzing because someone told him she uses his name as the answer to the security question when she logs into her bank account.

We climb the stairs and stand behind the curtain, watching a drum tech get ready for Sabrina Carpenter's set. It's so loud, nobody out in the crowd can hear him whacking away on the snare drum. All around us, people are wearing light-up antlers and taking selfies and chanting for their favorite artist. Then the lights go down and the crowd starts screaming and we walk out into the ocean of energy. The Garden. There's no place like it.

The rest of the night is more of the same. More two-minute drive-by interviews in the Gift Lounge: Alessia Cara (my girl!) . . . Bazzi (my boy!) . . . G-Eazy (he's so tall!) . . . Camila Cabello (my little sis!)—one after another, the stars hop up on my little stage, and I do my best to ask them something meaningful in the short time we have before they're swept away to the next thing. More quick onstage appearances to introduce an act or a video greeting from

Mariah Carey. More hugs and selfies backstage while Andrew and Steven try to drag me away to wherever I'm supposed to be. Hey, it's Ryan Seacrest! (Hugs for the cameras.) Hey, it's the head of Sony! Hey, it's Santa again!

Steven has good news and bad news. The bad news is that Khalid isn't feeling it tonight—no interview there. But Cardi B agreed to let us interview her in her dressing room. I've never met her, and she's tonight's headliner.

First, though, I get to hang out with Camila Cabello and a sleigh full of puppies. This is for the CW broadcast. The idea, as a producer quickly explains to me in a crowded hallway, is that Camila and I are going to exchange gifts. I am giving her a Harry Potter bathrobe, the producer explains (which is news to me, but I know she loves Harry Potter). It's already wrapped and waiting for me inside the room where they're taping. And there are two unbelievably small and cute French bulldog puppies in a stroller. "You can play with them if you want," the producer says.

Inside, Monét X Change from *RuPaul's Drag Race* is waiting in the sleigh. Camila comes in, and even though we've already done two other interviews tonight, we greet each other for the cameras. She's already performed twice tonight, once with Bazzi and once on her own, wearing something different and spectacular each time. I have no idea how she's still awake, let alone full of energy. She gives me her gift, which turns out to be a cute pair of mugs with my and Alex's names on them.

We play with the puppies. *Obviously.* We sing a few carols. And then we're off to the next place we're each supposed to be. Which for me is Cardi B's dressing room. She's got a 400-pound guy on one side of the door and a 350-pound guy on the other side, but they turn out to be 750 pounds of friendly, and the interview goes great. I'm so grateful that she's up for this. Just this morning she was in court clearing up some trouble with the law, but she's ready to talk about her music and her holiday plans with her baby. It was a thrill to meet and speak with her.

In an hour or so, she's going to take the stage and bring the house down. By then, the record company executives will be closing down the open bar, the rest of my radio family will be fanned out across the city getting ready for our after-parties, and me? I'll be gone. I was in Dmitriy's SUV long ago. My work was done.

On the ride back downtown, I'm exhausted—ready to pass out in my glamoflage suit. I've been up since five thirty this morning, and I've been "on" almost that entire time. I can't remember if I've eaten anything today.

And if I have a smile on my face, it's not because I got to go backstage. It's because of something I saw while I was waiting in the wings for one of my onstage appearances.

We sold out the Garden tonight, including some seats that are actually *behind* the stage. As in, you can't see anything that's happening. All you see is the ugly part. The sound board. The lighting rig. The back of the rotating stage where they're taking apart the previous act's set and putting together the next one's. The only way you can even see the show is on a video screen that's mounted way up near the ceiling.

But way back there, in the shittiest possible seats, was a group of young girls. Were they complaining that they didn't have a better spot? Hell no. They were all dressed up and jumping up and down with excitement, and singing along at the top of their lungs. They knew every word of every song from every artist. In the ten minutes I was standing back there, I must have watched them take a thousand selfies. They were having the time of their lives.

That's the power of live music. That's what a concert can do. That's what Jingle Ball is all about. And that's why my advice to you is this: Never, ever go backstage.

When you go backstage, it's like finding out how a magician does his tricks. No, it's worse. It's like finding out how a magician does his tricks and then listening to him bitch about how much his magic wand cost and how his assistant forgot to get him pre-check on his flight. Once you've heard all that, he's no longer a magician. He's just a guy.

We have so few opportunities in life to stop thinking about the boring but necessary work we have to do to get from one day to the next: Go to work, go grocery shopping, take out the trash, make that doctor's appointment. When you're at a concert, you can forget all that, if only for an hour and a half, and just disappear into the music. You can dream about standing up there with a guitar around your neck or a microphone in your hand, getting swept up in the roar of the crowd, letting the music just burst out from inside you. At a concert, everything feels larger than life. When the lights go down and the music starts, you suspend your disbelief and feel like anything's possible.

Going backstage may get you some free drinks and a chance to pose for a couple of fun pictures, but it pops that balloon and reminds you that even the most fun things in the world are somebody's job. And even if you could live out that rock-and-roll fantasy, you'd probably find out pretty quickly that it comes with its own annoyances and hassles.

Despite how exhausting it is, Jingle Ball is one of my favorite nights of the year. But I'll enjoy it a whole lot more when I can watch it from out there in the crowd.

CHAPTER 14

How to Be Famous

When it comes to pop music, we don't just fall in love with songs we hear on the radio. We fall in love with the artists who make them. Sure, the music itself might be what first catches our eye (*ear*). But there's so much more to the package.

Think about Lady Gaga. It all starts with the talent. She's such an amazing artist. If you heard just one of her songs—never saw her face, never knew her story—you'd be blown away.

But when you think about Gaga, you're not just thinking about how great "Bad Romance" is. You're thinking about the outrageous costumes she wears onstage, and the personal message her music sends to people, and the way she's always been so open and honest about her journey, and the courage she shows every time she peels off another layer.

There's a difference between being a musician and being a *star*. When you're a star, it's not just about the songs anymore. We follow you on social media. We obsess about who you're dating and how much you weigh and whether you're partying too much. You're still you, but you're also something more. An image. A *brand*.

I don't mean to sound cynical about this. Image is part of the show. Think about it this way: If you were a chef, and you made the world's most delicious lasagna, would you just plop a big scoop of it into a paper bowl and toss it on the table?

No. You would plate it carefully so it looks great on Instagram, and garnish it with micro-basil, and serve it in a restaurant you'd worked hard to design just the right way. And if you had a great story about how it was your nonna's recipe, and how the tomatoes came all the way from some tiny little village in Sicily, you'd make sure your customers knew about it.

And if you did it that way—if you worked to deliver a whole lasagna *experience* and not just a plate of food—would that make the lasagna itself any less impressive? Would it mean you weren't a *real chef* but instead some kind of *phony*? Of course not!

Shit. Now I'm hungry. Where was I? Oh, right. So, there's the person, and then there's the pop star. There's Stefani Germanotta, the incredibly talented musician and artist who grew up in New York. And then there's *Lady Gaga*, the pop star.

Or take Marshmello, another one of my favorites. Not only does he write and produce with the most talented in the business, he also performs at massive, fan-filled festivals with a giant marshmallow on his head. But if you follow him on social media, you can tell there's a real person in there: someone positive and inspirational and full of joy.

With that helmet on, he's performing even when he's not moving a muscle—there's art just in the way he looks. But on the other hand, without the helmet? No matter what he's doing, he's not *Marshmello* without it. One time I was at Jingle Ball in Miami and got a text from him: *Come say hi!* So I went back to his dressing room, the security guy let me in, and there was Marshmello—without his marshmallow. It was like walking in on your mom when she's just stepped out of the shower. I had to bite my tongue to stop myself from asking him if he could please put his head on.

I'm such a fan of his. When we were planning our wedding, Alex and I agreed on two things. One, we would love to have him DJ. Two, there was no way we could afford him. "Well," said Alex, "can't we just get a guy and put him in a marshmallow helmet? Would anyone know the difference?"

You know what? I actually think they would. Besides, I would never, ever, ever cheat someone I respect that much. Although, Marshmello, if you're reading this, maybe we can negotiate something for our anniversary party?

We're all fascinated by the relationship between real people and the stars they become. We all want to catch Clark Kent changing into the Superman tights. That's why meet-and-greets are so popular. We want to feel like we've gotten to know the artists on a *personal* level, like we've met the real person behind the image.

But here's the thing. By the time the meet-and-greet starts, Clark Kent has already taken off the glasses and put on the red pajamas. You get whisked out of your dressing room at *exactly* 7:01 and ushered into a cave full of fluorescent lights with a backdrop that has the name of whatever radio station or energy drink

ELVIS DURAN

paid to be a sponsor. There's a line of excited fans. And even if you're tired, or fighting off a cold, or constipated because you haven't had a green vegetable since your tour left the West Coast, you've got to be *on* from the minute you walk into the room. Nobody wants to wait in line to find out that their favorite pop star is having a shitty day.

So you're in there for eight minutes, and you take dozens of pictures, and you sign posters, and—even if, again, you *love* meeting fans—you're not going to remember anyone's name or be able to focus on the story they're telling about how they played your song at prom, or how their brother has a huge crush on you, or how they named their cat after your drummer. You're already thinking ahead to 7:09, when you're going to get whisked *out* of the room to go do something else.

Oh, and: Don't forget to smile.

The truth is, pop stars never really *get* to just be their real selves. They're expected to be *in character* all the time: sweet and romantic, or sassy and fun, or sexy and controversial, whatever the image is. But we *also* expect them to be *authentic*. If you found out that Lil Wayne has never done drugs even once in his entire life, you wouldn't just be surprised. You'd feel *cheated*.

They say, "Never meet your idols." I don't really buy that. The day I met Howard was one of the greatest days of my life. He's just so fucking cool. But on the other hand, the day I met Barry Manilow was a huge disappointment. He acted like such an a-hole. But maybe that isn't fair to him. Maybe he's just a crotchety old man who makes beautiful, romantic music. And maybe I should just enjoy the music instead of complaining in a book that he was a dick to me the one time we met.

But that's the job: Not only do you have to be talented, you have to (need to) create a public image that sells music, and live it twenty-four hours a day, seven days a week. And it has to be a *fun* image (because nobody likes boring celebrities) but also an *authentic* image (because nobody likes a phony).

One of the best parts of my job is that I get to know these artists *before* they get famous, when it's still all about the music and before the brand sets in. I saw a 5 Seconds of Summer video the other day, and it hit me: I knew these guys when they were a foot shorter. That's why I love doing that New Artist of the Month segment on the *Today* show: Before all the pressures of fame, you can see the passion for the music shine through.

At our iHeart studios, there's this little performance space called the Dunkin' Donuts Iced Coffee Lounge (how glamorous!) where artists on the rise come and perform for the tastemakers who work in the building. I can't imagine a more difficult audience—it's, like, ten thirty in the morning and you're playing for a dozen ad execs in business casual texting their assistants alongside the younger, fun assistants who broke away for a moment to enjoy some music.

But that's how we got to know Alessia Cara. Steven had heard that she was getting a lot of buzz, not just from our record industry friends, but among fans online, so we made sure to pay attention when she came in.

I wish I could tell you what the magic recipe is, what makes the difference between a talented artist and a star, but whatever it is, she had it. That much was clear right away. And it wasn't just her music. It was the way she wove herself into every song, and the way you could see in every interaction that she wasn't putting on a front. She's so self-deprecating and charming and down-to-earth. You just want to root for her.

On the other hand, Bebe Rexha—stunning, confident, she *owns* the stage the minute she steps onto it. But she's still fun and funny and humble. Like a lot of artists, she grew up listening to us in Staten Island, and you could tell right away what it meant to her to be on our show. She even brought her parents into the interview, and every time we talked about her music, her dad would start crying with pride.

Two very different artists, and just a couple of the dozens and dozens I've had the privilege of introducing to the country as an Artist of the Month on the *Today* show.

Sometimes, with the artists we meet, that's as far as it goes.

But for the lucky few—the ones who find themselves on a path to true superstardom—life gets a lot more complicated in a hurry.

Imagine you've been writing songs in your bedroom since you were seven years old, plinking away on an electronic keyboard, singing into your hairbrush, putting on shows for your family. It's your passion.

So you buy a copy of GarageBand, and you record some songs, and you put them up on SoundCloud and send links around to your friends. Someone leaves a nice comment, and you feel good about it all day. And then you go to your day job, the one that pays the rent so you can keep writing music in your free time.

Then one morning you wake up and your song has three hundred thousand views on YouTube. And your Twitter is going nuts. And there's a message on your phone from someone at an *actual record company.*

Holy *shit*.

Soon, you're recording your song in a real studio, and they're playing it on Z100, and I'm introducing you on live national television. And then you get a record deal, and you get to put out a whole album, and you go from playing at open mics to playing at Madison Square fucking Garden.

Artists blow up like that all the time these days. But when it finally happens to you, you suddenly find yourself surrounded by all these voices telling you what you're supposed to do next.

Endorse this product! Work with this producer! Go on this show! Change your hair! Change your outfit! Change your sound! Get a makeover! Get a nose job! Get a tummy tuck!

Meet your new media coach, your new stylist, your new publicist. Oh, and your new security detail—you don't want to know why we decided we had to hire those guys. Here's your financial adviser and your tour manager and your mindfulness guru and ten thousand guys from the record company who all kind of look the same and you'll never in a million years remember what each one of them is doing to help you sell your album!

We're flying you to Paris for Fashion Week! We're sending you to Los Angeles to work with Mark Ronson! We're booking you on *Saturday Night Live*! You've got a hundred interviews to prep for and a thousand posters to sign and a million people tweeting at you, and, oh, by the way, how's that new album coming?

Everybody has something to offer you. Everybody wants something in return. You're constantly having to decide when to say yes and when to say no. Oh, and, by the way, you're no longer just an *artist*—you're a *business*. All these people around you? They're *relying* on you to feed their families. So while you might fantasize about taking the money you made from that hot debut single and vanishing into the witness protection program, you feel like you can't let them down.

In the movies, idealistic young artists get corrupted by drug abuse and jealous fights with bandmates and evil record company executives. And that kind of drama does happen sometimes. But more often the thing that winds up sidetracking young stars is the simple fact that if you want to be successful, you have to do lots of stuff that has nothing to do with the art you got into this business to create and share.

The red carpet is a good example. It looks like fun, right? And if you're not one of the artists walking it, it really is. (If you ever get a chance to go backstage, skip it—but if you ever get a chance to hang out on a red carpet, *do it.*)

I first got to do the Grammy red carpet in 2014. It was another Steven Levine brainstorm. I'd been doing backstage interviews for *Extra* and *Entertainment Tonight* forever, and when Steven would talk with the producers of these shows, which were owned by CBS, he would always put in a plug for me to take my talents to another CBS property: the Grammy Awards.

Finally, they agreed. So I squeezed myself into a tuxedo and hit the red carpet alongside Nancy O'Dell. Because we were working for CBS, the network that hosts the Grammys, we were in what's known as "first position"—the very first stop on the red carpet. I tried my best to be a friendly face, to put people at ease, even as, in the corner of my eye, I watched Steven racing back and forth, wrangling the wranglers and lining up our next interview.

What a trip. I felt like a kid in a candy store. I'd be standing there talking to Neil Patrick Harris and his husband, and then Madonna would come up behind him, and then Taylor Swift would be popping out of a limo, and, whoa, there's *Oprah!*

And *everyone* is fired up. There is an undeniable energy to the red carpet. Imagine it from the stars' point of view. You've spent months working with your fashion team and famous designers figuring out the *perfect* dress. And then, on the day of the show, you often have to get up early so you can be *sewn into* it—and then spend hours on hair and makeup. Then you—*very carefully*—pack yourself into the back of an SUV with your date and your publicist and your manager for the ride to the theater. And when that SUV pulls up in front of the red carpet, you are *on*—because the press is *right there*, already taking pictures. Which means you have to get out of that SUV *very, VERY carefully* (it's way easier for men).

You barely have time to register that the red carpet isn't red at all—it's more like fuchsia, but it reads as red on TV—because, unlike at your concerts, where you come in via the loading dock and wander the concrete hallways on the way to your dressing room, you're *already onstage*. The camera flashes are *blinding*. Everyone is yelling your name, asking—well, "asking" is too polite, try "demanding"—that you turn *this way* and *that way* and *smile* and *pose*.

I've walked a red carpet or two in my time. Usually at an iHeartRadio event. And, even there, nobody gets *too* excited to see me walking by. Still, I get nervous about it. And I can only imagine what it's like to be Selena Gomez or Justin Timberlake at the Grammys. I know of several artists who've burst into tears with the anxiety of it all and run back to their SUV. And there *is* always a back entrance for celebrities who just can't bring themselves to go through the whole ordeal, either because they're shy or because they're in the middle of some bad press.

But your record company wants you to walk that fucking carpet—where, by the way, there's always the chance that, somewhere in that gauntlet of light and noise, someone's going to *create* some bad press for you.

The second year I did the red carpet, Nancy and I were talking to Taylor Swift, who'd been in all the tabloids because of her dating life. We were *trying* to keep it focused on the music, but Nancy goofed.

"You're going to walk away with maybe more than just a trophy tonight, I think, lots of men."

The *look* Taylor gave her. I almost melted into my shoes. She handled it pretty well: "I'm gonna go hang out with my friends, and then I go home to my cats." But it made all kinds of headlines the next day, Taylor giving Nancy the death glare while I tried not to cringe. It wound up being the last time I did the Grammy red carpet.

By the way, while all this was going on, I saw Katy Perry out of the corner of my eye—and watched her walk *right past us.* Later, she got in touch to apologize . . . and that's when we found out that she and Taylor were rumored to be feuding. But that's another story.

Fame isn't a ladder. It's an escalator. Once you get on, it's impossible to get off—and it's hard to even pause for half a second and reflect on where you are and where you're going.

Every artist deals with all this pressure in a different way. Taylor Swift, for example—she surrounds herself with layers and layers of people she trusts to make sure nobody gets too close. For the record, I don't blame her. People treat her horribly. And everyone has a right to feel safe and comfortable.

But sometimes I wonder if building those walls around yourself is really the best way to go. We deal with artists' "people" all the time, and while a lot of them are great, some are real pains in the ass. I can't tell you how many times we've asked an artist's publicist for an interview, and they'll put us off forever, and then later I'll run into the artist at an event or something and find out that the request never even got through to them.

Most of the celebrities I don't get along with, it's probably because of their "people." I'm tempted to name names. But you would only know the star's name, not the name of the publicist who never returns our phone calls but always shows up in our inbox when they want us to add their client's latest song to our playlist. And judging an artist by the jackass she hired just isn't fair.

Like I said, I can't blame anyone who feels like they need to hide behind a moat to protect their image. But I have noticed that a lot of the artists who've been around for a long time are much more relaxed. They don't travel with a big posse. They're okay letting their guard down in public. Artists like Paul McCartney and Sting—they seem so much more chill, and so much happier.

That's why Gaga is one of my all-time favorites. The first time I met her was backstage at her first Jingle Ball. She wasn't really on the map yet, but she had on this amazing outfit and four-inch eyelashes and these crazy shoes. *Wow.*

So then she put out her debut album with all those hits. It sounded so great. All those dancy, poppy, feel-good hits. And they were totally aligned with her image. Every time she walked out onto a stage, everything from her look to the staging told you that she was *owning* her image. She was a walking art gallery. I loved it.

But she's never felt like she was a prisoner to her own early success. She's always felt free to follow her gut and her talent. And that lets her do amazing things. Duet with Tony Bennett? Star in a movie? Work with visual artists instead of just making another album? Gaga knows exactly who she is. And she works through the doubts. It's always just her, and her paintbrush, and her fucking canvas.

Another one of my favorites is Demi Lovato. Gaga and Demi are very different people, and very different artists, who have had very different experiences in the spotlight. But you can tell how much they care about their work by how much of themselves they put into it—and how fearless they are in letting the world follow along on their journeys.

You might think Demi's story is that of someone who got eaten up by pressure, given what she's gone through in recent years. But I think she's one of the most courageous artists I've ever met. The way she's shared her struggles with her fans, and used them to make her music more personal and honest—it makes her art mean something more.

It also makes me feel protective of her. She once did a show at the iHeartRadio Theater, and before she went on, her manager told me she'd been having trouble with her voice. She even warned the crowd that she might not be at the top of her game. Could have fooled me—she sounded beautiful, as always. Still, by the end of her set, she was struggling.

The script called for me to walk out onstage and set up her big encore, but something in me just clenched up, so when I got out there, I asked for one more big standing ovation, thanked the crowd for coming, and whispered to Demi, "You're good."

She was confused. Even though she was exhausted, she was ready to push through for the encore. But we whisked her out.

Later, I texted Demi to explain. I worried she might be upset that we called it a night on her behalf. But she texted right back to put my mind at ease, explaining that there's nothing worse for a singer than trying to perform without a voice and thanking me for pulling her offstage. Phew.

I don't have that kind of relationship with every artist. Most of the time, even when we enjoy each other's company, the relationship is professional. But that's impossible with Demi. She lives out loud, too, and you can't help but feel a personal connection. The day we heard she'd been rushed to the hospital after an overdose, I felt like I'd been punched in the gut. After hours of waiting—agony—we finally heard she was going to be okay. Thank God—she was somewhere getting the help she deserved.

One thing that seems to help is having a strong support system— one that isn't on your payroll. Miley Cyrus is one of those artists who seems to have figured out a way to be in the spotlight without losing her sense of self. She's so honest and so open and so free. And I think a lot of that comes from having a family she's close to—her mom even comes on the road with her.

When I think of the artists I never have to worry about—the ones who seem to have figured out how to be famous while still keeping their feet under them—it's usually the ones who have introduced me to their parents. You meet Meghan Trainor's dad, and you know she's going to be okay. You meet Sabrina Carpenter's mom, and you know she's going to be okay.

Of course, even when you're a well-adjusted person with a strong family, being famous has its ups and downs. I've been friends with Camila Cabello since she was in Fifth Harmony—a group we really loved having on the show. I'd always see her backstage at shows, and her mother and grandmother would be there, and it always made me feel confident that she'd be okay.

But you could see that not everything was okay with the group. They did our Jingle Ball tour in 2016, so I saw them backstage at several different shows, and by the last stop on the tour—Miami—the tension was clear.

That night, I got a text from Camila asking me not to leave without stopping by her dressing room, because she needed to talk to me.

I told her I'd come by, and I meant it. But it was a crazy night, and I couldn't find my driver in all the chaos, and someone offered me a ride back to the hotel, and it just slipped my mind. Sitting in the backseat of the car, I got another text from Camila asking where I was.

I'm on my way back to the hotel.

Silence for a few minutes. Then, something like: *You said you were gonna come find me. I need to talk to you.*

I told her I was sorry. And right around then is when the fire-works began. A late-night press release came out saying she was leaving the group.

It got ugly at first. It was the kind of drama that could sidetrack someone's career. But I knew Camila, and I knew the other girls in the group. I knew how talented they were—and, what's more, I knew that they were tough enough to make it through all the bullshit and find ways to keep sharing that talent with all of us.

Sure enough, Camila's already putting out great songs on her own and getting more and more successful, with a mountain of Grammys on the way—and I'm confident that the rest of the group aren't far behind. They're all working hard and seeing results.

I know that the pop culture industry wants us to take sides—Nicki vs. Cardi, Katy vs. Taylor, Camila vs. the rest of Fifth Har-mony. But I really believe there's room for everyone.

Take One Direction. I used to love interviewing them as a group, because they were all so open and fun and easygoing—and they loved, loved, loved music. We could just sit around the table and talk about the craft and it felt like we'd known each other for a thousand years.

When they split up, everyone thought it would be drama and angst. But I knew it wouldn't be. I knew they each had something to contribute—and I've loved watching them all make their own way.

Speaking of breakups that turned out great: the Jonas Brothers. These three guys grew up together, became superstars before they could legally drink, and then they got sick of each other and everything fell apart. Not just the band—the *family*. I'd known them since the beginning, and it was heartbreaking to watch.

They each went their separate ways—Nick built his own career as a solo artist, Joe started a band with a whole different sound, and Kevin left the business altogether and started a family. They gave each other time and space to grow up on their own.

And so, when they started making a documentary about the lives they'd built separately, they started to realize that maybe they'd grown up enough that they could come back together. Not just as a family, but as the band that so many people loved.

"There was a magic together that we missed," Nick told us when they came on the show the day after they announced their reunion. I was so happy to see them so happy.

Families are tough. Breakups are tough. But these guys were tougher. What an incredible story. Go see them on tour if you can—you'll see what Nick meant by *magic*.

Sometimes it's hard to know how to be the right kind of supportive. You want these kids to succeed in the industry, but you don't want to push them when they're not ready to be pushed.

I'm thinking about Aaron Carter. He actually reached out to me to let me know he'd written some new music and ask if he could come on our show and perform it. So talented. We hadn't heard from him in a while. What we *had* heard were a bunch of tabloid stories about his breakup with his girlfriend, his sexuality, and his very public feud with his famous brother, Nick. People were going after him on social media, spreading ugly rumors. And it seemed like he was in a fragile spot. But we set it up anyway.

I was blown away by his courage. He let everything out. But he wound up breaking down in the middle of his performance.

And I wound up feeling like I'd let him down. It wasn't the right time to put him on the air. I still hate thinking back on all the buzzy gossip stories that came out of that interview. Aaron is so talented. His story should be about his talent, not all the other bullshit. Luckily, as I write this, he seems to be on a brighter path. He deserves it!

Of course, if you're talking about someone who suffers from the fact that his art gets overlooked in favor of the rest of the image, you have to talk about Justin Bieber. I've known him since he was just a kid, been interviewing him for years. I feel like we've all watched him grow up.

He's always been a super-solid musician. But at first, a lot of his fan base came from the fact that he was young and cute, with the floppy hair and the high voice. And as he got older, and that image changed, people started to roll their eyes. They'd read a headline about how he was driving recklessly through the streets of Miami, or peeing in a janitor's mop bucket, or throwing eggs at a neighbor's house, and they'd get so focused on how he wasn't that cute little kid anymore, they'd miss the fact that he was still making incredible music. I always say that Justin has a mountain of talent. But that gets lost in all the other stuff.

I once interviewed him at my apartment in New York for *Entertainment Tonight*—and when *ET* comes over, they roll deep. I'm talking like a dozen people and case after case of lighting and sound equipment. My living room was chock-full of bodies and boxes.

Then Justin showed up with his manager, Scooter Braun, and their team. He wandered over to the huge catering spread I'd ordered and ate exactly one grape. Then I pulled him into a side bedroom with the excuse of giving him a pair of Alexander

McQueen sneakers I'd bought him as a gift. He said thanks. "Hey," I said, "do you just want to chill out in here while we get everything set up?" So he laid down on the bed and relaxed by himself. I wondered how many quiet moments like that he gets to experience.

I could tell the whole scene was kind of overwhelming, so Scooter shooed a dozen techies and producers upstairs to the roof terrace, leaving just a few downstairs for the actual interview. But even though we fixed the overcrowding problem, I had a sheet of questions prepared by the *ET* producers that I could tell right away would make him uncomfortable. Stuff about his parents, his relationships, his scandals. I felt terrible, but it clearly wasn't my interview.

When he left, I kept thinking about how hard it must be for him, to have every minute of his life be crowded and noisy and chaotic, to be picked apart for everything *but* the thing he was so great at, to constantly have to put on a happy face even when all he really wanted was to chill out for one second.

I've always wanted to apologize to Justin . . . and let him know that those weren't the questions I wanted to ask. Maybe putting it in this book will do it. But maybe he's already forgotten about it. God knows he's been faced with plenty of obnoxious interviews since then. And maybe the best way to apologize for something is to make a change as a result of your mistake.

So, Justin, if you're reading this, know that I'm sorry. But, more important, know this: Because of that day, I don't ask anyone else's questions anymore. I learned my lesson.

*　　*　　*

Don't get me wrong—hanging out with artists can be a lot of fun. Whenever I finally get driven into obscurity, I'll have lots of memories to giggle about with Alex while we watch the sunset from our rocking chairs.

One time, I was interviewing Bono backstage at a concert, and I think he could tell that I was *way* too excited about it, because in the middle of the interview he walked around behind me and started giving me a nice, calming shoulder massage. *I got a back rub from Bono*. I love just *saying* that.

Then there was the time I was going to do a TV interview with Rihanna backstage at the iHeartMusic Festival. It was total chaos—a million people running around in a million different directions—and then there was me, with my little microphone, waiting patiently. When she came off the stage, though, she found me instantly and took my hand.

"Elvis," she said, in that elegant Rihanna voice, "take me to my trailer." Yes, I said *trailer*. Rihanna doesn't settle for a dressing *room*. Even at an indoor venue.

So I did, but we were instantly swarmed with people trying to get to her. So what did Rihanna do? She jumped on my back and started slapping me on the ass like I was a racehorse. And what did I do? Well, I gave her a piggyback ride to her trailer, obviously. It wound up being a great interview.

And, of course, there are all the stories that involve copious amounts of drinking. I feel like it's probably not a good thing that lots of the drinking stories happened during my radio show, which, just to remind you, takes place at *six o'clock in the morning*.

French Montana came in one day, and I forget why, but we started doing tequila shots. Not just *a* tequila shot, like, "Ha-ha, we're drinking in the morning." A *series* of tequila shots, like, "I need to not remember this day." French is a big guy, of course, so he could handle his liquor, which was good, because he had more press appearances to do later in the morning. I am not a big guy, at least not anymore. The rest of that day is pretty blurry for me.

There are certain artists who bring it out in me. Jason Derulo is definitely one. We've done shots on the air together. Shaggy is another. We always have cocktails, and he even brought us a bottle of his own Shaggy cognac (we served it to Ed Sheeran on another show and got him pretty lit). Then there is the time I found myself smoking cigars with Nick and Joe Jonas alongside Charlie Puth while we tooled around an after-party in Miami on the back of a Vespa. Hopefully nobody has pictures.

But moments like those—moments where everybody can let their hair down and just have fun—are the exception, not the rule, both for me and for the artists we work with.

That's why I care so much about making our show a comfortable place for the performers we have on. I don't want to *catch* them picking their nose or being exhausted after a year of touring or wishing they could just go back to playing in front of tiny crowds who don't know their name. I want them to feel comfortable *telling* us that stuff.

On our show, we don't pretend that being a pop star is all glitz and glamour. We know that it's a job just like anyone else's. We love all the work these artists do to bring us their music, but we also want them to feel free to be real people, too.

And the cool thing is, that approach doesn't just work for pop stars. It works for all of us. We all work so hard to be the people we expect ourselves to be. Not just at our jobs, but in our relationships and with our families. We're all playing characters. That's what this busy, pressure-packed world expects of us.

But what if we gave ourselves space to put down the masks, just for a little while? What if we sought out people and places that made us feel free to be who we are, not who we think we have to be? What if we judged *ourselves* by our talent, and not by how well we play the game society wants us to play? What if we all admitted that while we spend all day playing Superman, we're all just itching to get out of those tights and go back to being Clark Kent?

Life is hard. We're all on an escalator. We're all under pressure. And I think it's important that we take time to hit pause, take a breath, and love ourselves without measuring ourselves against all those expectations.

Yes, my message in this chapter is that we should be a little less judgmental about our favorite artists. But let's not forget to be a little less judgmental about ourselves, too. Even if we're not famous. Yet.

And okay, maybe there's a little lesson for myself in here, too. For all the complaining I do about how busy I am and how cutthroat the radio business can be and how much backstage sucks, all the things I hate about my job are things that allow me to do the show every day—the thing I love more than anything else. If Justin Bieber can handle it, why can't I?

CHAPTER 15

Dr. Oz Saves My Life

There's nothing better than a birthday party at the office. Well, if you work in *my* office, that is. We don't do stale donuts and awkward singing in the break room. We throw *down*. And when I turned fifty in the summer of 2014, my family at Z100 really went all out.

Champagne. Balloons. A crazy, multilevel cake, plus three kinds of cupcakes, and if that wasn't enough sugar, a whole table covered in candy.

Greg T wore a top hat and tails. Mr. Met dropped by, giant baseball head and all. Mayor Bill de Blasio issued a special proclamation declaring August 5, 2014, to be Elvis Duran Day in New York City. A whole bunch of my celebrity friends—everyone from Lady Gaga to Katy Perry to Bruno Mars—were kind enough to record a video birthday card. And yes, there were puppies.

It was incredible to be showered with love by so many of the people who meant the most to me. But I look back at the pictures from that day and I can't help but cringe a little. There's a smile on my face in all the shots where I'm posing with a slice of cake or an elaborately wrapped present, but it's mouth only. You can tell there's something not quite right.

Lots of my well-wishers joked that I didn't *look* fifty. Maybe not. But I didn't look *good.* I didn't *feel* good. After a lifetime of trying—and mostly failing—to keep my weight under control, I had ballooned to 260 pounds. It was the heaviest I'd ever been. And on what should have been one of the happiest days of my life, it was, I guess you could say, weighing heavily on my mind.

Here's the thing. I *love* food. *Love* it. I love to cook (when I have time, which is never, which is why the apartment is littered with all sorts of kitchen gadgets still in their original packaging). In fact, I'm tempted to switch gears right now and turn the rest of this book into a cookbook (*Where Do I Begin?* With the bread basket, obviously!). Let me tell you about my stuffed-pepper recipe. You take a pound of ground turkey, and you—

Okay, no. That would be a cheat. I said I was going to tell you everything, so here goes.

The truth is, the story of Heavy Elvis isn't a story about a guy who liked food *too much.* As far as I'm concerned, there's no such *thing* as liking food too much. Food is so closely linked to history, to tradition. You can actually taste enlightenment and knowledge. I've always been a fan of great food and great chefs, and I always will be. No matter how much I weigh.

But while my relationship with food is as passionate today as it's ever been, that relationship used to be a lot less healthy.

Despite all my awesome, supportive friends . . . despite all the awards and accolades . . . despite the fact that I literally *perform for an audience* for a living—I've always had a problem with confidence. And for a long time, that was closely related to the problem I had with my weight. Some people only need food for fuel. I wonder what that's like! Me, I needed it as a distraction, as a companion, and, most of all, as a security blanket. Whenever I felt tense or vulnerable, bored or alone, I'd find myself in front of the refrigerator. And, of course, it was a vicious cycle: The more I ate, the worse I felt, and so . . . the more I ate.

I guess I'm two different kinds of big eater. There's the kind who loves going out with friends and having a great meal, is always down to split an appetizer or three, and can't say no to a bite of your dessert. I'll always be that guy.

But then there's the kind of eater who eats because he's anxious, because he had a bad day at work, or even just because he doesn't know what to do with himself and happens to wander past the fridge while pacing his apartment. I'm that guy, too. I have been ever since I was that weird, loner kid who came home from school to an empty house and, not knowing what else to do and not having anyone else to talk to, would polish off a pound of spaghetti as an afternoon snack.

When I was younger, my weight fluctuated a lot. I'd have a rough patch, and my pants would start getting tight, so I'd drink vodka sodas instead of margaritas and maybe go for a run a couple times a week, and I'd slim down a bit. But as I got older, my metabolism disappeared, and it got a lot easier to put weight on and a lot harder to take it off. I tried Weight Watchers, and it worked! A little. For a while. But I always would end up falling off the wagon sooner or later (usually carb-related).

By the time I was fifty, I hated the way I looked in pictures. I hated the feeling of dread that would come over me whenever Steven lined up a chance for me to be on TV. I hated walking up a flight of stairs and realizing that somehow, that tiny bit of exertion had caused me to sweat through my shirt.

For God's sake, I'd look down and not be able to see my wiener!

But the thing I hated most of all was getting dressed.

I love clothes almost as much as I love food. But every time I opened up my closet to pick something out for an appearance, my heart would sink. Instead of trying to decide what look I wanted to go for that night, I was just trying to find something—anything—that still fit. Or I'd go shopping and see all this great stuff at Saks Fifth Avenue, only for the salesman to tell me, as politely as he could, that it didn't come in my size. I have so many memories of straining to button a shirt, or sucking in my gut on the red carpet, or hoping against hope my seams wouldn't split when I got out of the car.

And, of course, after a night of feeling uncomfortable, the only thing that would make me feel better would be . . . yup—eating something indulgent.

So, my body-image situation was . . . not great. And while, as you've seen, I took kind of a devil-may-care approach to my physical well-being in general in my younger years, by the time I turned fifty, I wasn't really enjoying treating my body like an amusement park anymore.

In fact, I was feeling sick and worn down all the time. I wasn't sleeping well. Plus, I'd just lost both of my parents within a matter of months after watching their health deteriorate for years: Dad had lost his eyesight to macular degeneration and suffered from COPD after decades of smoking, and Mom had fallen prey to dementia. Neither one of them ever took great care of themselves—we weren't a big exercise family—and watching their bodies fail them after they retired drove home the point that the human body comes with an expiration date, and if I wasn't careful, mine might be sooner than I thought.

I'd known Dr. Oz—his first name is Mehmet, but nobody uses it—for years, but only professionally. He's a great radio guest. Super smart, quick-witted, but always compassionate and supportive. Our audience loves him. And, even better, they *trust* him. I guess that's down to what doctors would call his *bedside manner* (that term always makes me giggle).

Anyway, one day, he was coming on to talk about the importance of regular checkups, and we thought, just for the hell of it, we'd have him check everyone's blood pressure right there in the studio, live on the air. So he went around the room with the little cuff, squeezed the little rubber ball, and gave everyone their reading: Danielle, Skeery, Greg T—and then he got to me. He looked at the dial, said something casual—"Oh, okay, you're all right"—and moved on.

Kinda weird, I thought, but we were coming up on a hard out, so I threw it to break.

As is usually the case during commercials, the studio got noisy fast, with people running in and out to deliver messages, Danielle gossiping with Nate, Greg T yelling at Skeery about whatever dumb thing they were at each other's throats about that day. But Dr. Oz put his hand on my arm and leaned in close, looking me right in the eyes.

"Look," he said. "I didn't want to say anything on the air, but, um, you should probably be in the hospital right now."

Say what?

"Your blood pressure," he said. "It's *crazy* high. Here, let me take it again, just to be sure."

It all got real. Real fast.

He strapped the cuff back around my arm. He watched the dial. I watched his face. Neither one of us liked what we saw.

"Okay, yeah," he said, shaking his head. "I'm seriously thinking about driving you to the ER right now."

I was more shocked than I was surprised. I mean, I obviously knew I was overweight, and I knew it was getting worse by the month. I knew it wasn't good for me. But I'd never had the Big Scare, the come-to-Jesus moment. The closest I ever got to reckoning with what I was doing to my body would be when I'd outgrow another suit jacket, and even then I could just blame it on the dry cleaner and send it off to Goodwill.

But here, now, with an ad for mufflers, or Edible Arrangements, or whatever blaring in the background—here was that moment. And sometimes I think about what might have happened if we'd had a different guest in the studio, or if we hadn't decided to do that little blood-pressure stunt, or if Dr. Oz hadn't been the kind of friend, and the kind of person, who would say something in a situation like that, even if it was awkward.

Would I have eaten myself into a heart attack and had an epiphany in the recovery room about how valuable life is and how I needed to finally get serious about my weight? Would I have even made it to the recovery room at all?

There's that old saying about how if you drop a frog into a pot of boiling water, he'll jump right out—but if you put him in a pot of cold water and then put it on the stove, he'll just sit there and slowly cook to death. Sometimes in life it's hard to tell that the water around you is heating up. Maybe you have a job that's crushing your soul, or maybe you're in a relationship that's turning toxic, or maybe you, too, have a health problem you're not taking care of—whatever it is, it happens slowly and gradually enough that you might just sit there and boil unless you have a friend who's brave enough and compassionate enough to say something.

Ever since the day Dr. Oz saved my life, I've tried to collect and treasure friends like that. I've tried to *be* a friend like that.

But first I had to lose some damn weight.

I figured Dr. Oz would tell me to buy a treadmill and cut back on the chicken parm. But instead he told me to go talk to Dr. Marc Bessler, a friend of his at NewYork-Presbyterian in Manhattan who specialized in weight-loss surgery. He was even kind enough to call ahead to make sure I could get in for an appointment (or maybe to make sure I *went*).

It's crazy—even at my heaviest, I had never imagined that I might be a candidate for that kind of procedure. A close friend had undergone the surgery just a couple of years earlier, and he'd even suggested, gently, that I look into it. But I didn't think I was fat enough.

Dr. Bessler disagreed, to put it mildly. The word *morbidly* got thrown around a lot. And then came a whole bunch of tests. The very first cardiogram showed a huge black spot on my heart, as if part of it had just shut down and died. I was terrified—but it turned out to just be a shadow.

Still, in the weeks that followed, there were a lot more EKGs, and a lot of needles, and a lot of stress tests. I even had to do one of those sleep studies, where they strap a mask on your face and attach electrodes to your balls like you're being tortured in a spy movie and then turn off the lights and encourage you to "sleep normally." *Yeah, right.*

The tests showed that I would be a good candidate for a bariatric sleeve procedure, where they basically cut a chunk out of your stomach—less stomach space, less room for food, fewer calories in your body, less weight. I was relieved that they weren't recommending the other procedure, the one that made Al Roker shit his pants at the White House. But I was still pretty nervous about making the decision.

Alex and I spent a lot of late nights talking about it. When we'd met, he was one of those hard-bodied club kids. A lot of his friends gave him grief for going out with an older and, uh, *softer* guy. It didn't exactly help my self-confidence.

But it did give me a lot of confidence in the relationship Alex and I were building. He always brushed off the jokes. And I always knew that he loved me—even when I didn't really like the way I looked. What's more, he loved me for *me.* Not for money or fame (which is good, because by celebrity standards I can't offer a whole lot of either). Not for my looks. He didn't have an agenda. I knew he would be with me through thick and thin—pun intended.

As we talked over every facet of the decision, I realized how lucky I was to have Alex in my life—not just a boyfriend, but a true *partner.* People spend decades looking for a relationship like that. Some never find it. And, I realized, if I was lucky enough to be able to build a life with someone I truly loved and trusted, someone who appreciated me and accepted me and who would support me through anything, why wouldn't I do everything in my power to make sure that life was as long and as healthy as possible?

Alex agreed. He didn't make a big deal about me being fat. But he cared a whole lot about me maybe not being *around*.

So I went back in to see Dr. Bessler, and as soon as he came into the room, I told him I'd made up my mind. I wanted to have the surgery. He was a little surprised by my quick decision, but he had the next steps ready: a *few* more tests and then submit a *few* more forms and then he was pretty sure he could get my insurance to cover it.

Nope, I said. I'm doing it. I don't care about the insurance.

"But we're talking about tens of thousands of dollars," he protested.

I repeated that I didn't care.

"Okay," he said, a little dubiously. "You sure you don't want to wait for the last batch of results from that sleep study?"

"Screw it. I'll sign a waiver or something."

I explained that, the way I make decisions, I needed to be impulsive. Otherwise, I'd be liable to chicken out. So I took out my phone, opened my calendar, and nodded at the leather book on his desk.

"Let's find a date and schedule it."

We settled on December 22, figuring I could use our show's Christmas break to recover from the procedure, and shook hands. I walked out of his office having signed a new lease on life.

Leading up to a bariatric sleeve procedure, you have to eat a special diet to prepare your body for the surgery. But that was the easy part. Preparing my *mind* for it was harder. As the nurses prepped me for the procedure, I found myself suddenly getting emotional.

One of the nurses saw a tear in my eye and asked me what was wrong. I didn't know quite how to put it into words.

"It's just . . . weird," I finally said. "I've had this same stomach since I was *born*. And now you guys are about to take some of it *out*."

She smiled at me. "That's pretty common," she said. And pretty soon, I was breathing into a mask, and counting backward from a hundred, and . . .

I woke up dizzy and annoyed. Dizzy because of the anesthetic. Annoyed because of my roommate.

When Dr. Bessler had told me that I'd need to spend the night in the hospital, I'd immediately gone Full Diva and said I'd pay for a private room. Unfortunately, none were available. Maybe if I'd been an *actual* diva. I doubt Mariah ever had to share a room.

Anyway, I wound up having to share with this guy who was

just kind of a mess. I think he had some mental health issues to go along with whatever physical ailment had brought him into the ICU. He lived in a halfway house, which I knew because he wouldn't stop talking to me. And I would have tried to be sympathetic, or at least polite, but all I wanted to do was lie there in peace and watch the ceiling spin. I kept jamming on the morphine button, hoping to knock myself out before I had to hear more complaints about the guy's bedsores, which he kept trying to show me.

I didn't sleep well the first night after the surgery. How *could* I, with all those machines beeping, and the guy next to me yelling, and the nurses coming in every twenty minutes—they'd *wake me up* to give me *sleeping pills*—but the next day was a little better. It's incredible how they can cut out a hunk of an important internal organ and then forty-eight hours later you're a little sore and very tired . . . but otherwise ready to get back to your life.

Well, a *different* life. People sometimes think that weight-loss surgery is "taking the easy way out," but there's nothing easy about it. You *do* lose a bunch of weight pretty quickly. But if you don't do the work to change your lifestyle, you won't keep it off—something I'm currently struggling with. Lots of people have the surgery only to gain back every pound—and then some. Nothing's guaranteed.

For the first few weeks after the surgery, you can't eat anything solid. Liquids only. And none of the fun ones that mix well with triple sec.

Alex and I had rented a place in Miami Beach for the week between Christmas and New Year's—a huge mansion, right on the water. And of course we invited Uncle Johnny to come along. Because nothing says "quiet" and "restful" like Uncle Johnny.

But we couldn't leave until the twenty-sixth, because Alex had to work all the way through Christmas Day. I woke up on Christmas morning and found myself alone in our apartment, three days removed from surgery, still feeling a little woozy. I looked down at my body and wondered what was going to happen to it. Thank God for Linda, one of my best friends. She called and said, "It's time to get you out of the house." So we got on an uptown train and sat by the East River, near Sutton Place, drinking hot tea, not saying much, just watching the world go by. I'll remember that Christmas day for a long, long time.

Our week in Miami I'll also remember. But not quite as pleasurably. I kind of knew it was going to be a mess. Everyone was very supportive and understood that I had to take it easy—but, come on, Miami is Miami, and nobody *really* felt like ministering to the patient, not when there were bars to crawl and friends to party with. Alex and Uncle Johnny gamely tried to hang out with me, mixing martinis at the house while I mixed protein shakes, but the drunker they got, the more restless they got. Miami was calling! Eventually, I just told them: "*Go* already."

I was bored, too. No martinis for me. No bars for me. Just medicine. And even that was a pain. See, you can't swallow pills right after this surgery, because your brand-new stomach isn't ready to handle even that small a chunk of solid material. I had these pills to keep my blood pressure down, and I had to crush them up and stir them into a glass of water. *Yum.*

Within a few days, I had had enough convalescence. One night we got Thai food, and I decided—doctor's advice or no doctor's advice—it was time to *chew*, dammit! I still remember the first thing I ate: an order of Massaman curry. Two bites in, I was completely full and ready to lie down—for some reason, I kept getting tired all of a sudden, almost to the point of fainting. Still, breaking the rules never tasted so good.

I had to do my New Year's toast with water—and not even *sparkling* water, because carbonation would do a number on my newly shrunk stomach. But I was excited to get back to my new life. And I was excited to share my journey with my audience when the show came back from the holiday break.

A lot of celebrities have had this surgery and kept quiet about it. They'll disappear from the scene for a few months, maybe with some excuse about "exhaustion," and then reemerge looking a hell of a lot skinnier, talking about how they cut out carbs and magically lost a hundred pounds.

I didn't want to do that. The relationship I have with my audience wouldn't work if I couldn't tell them about stuff like this. And after years of sharing everything from my deepest thoughts and feelings to my bowel movements, it would have felt weird to hide this.

But I didn't just want to *acknowledge* that I'd had the surgery. I wanted to *brag* about it.

I was excited about my new body. The weight was already coming off! There's a picture from that week in Miami where I'm holding up a lobster, and I already look a little thinner. Tired, but thinner.

And as excited as I was about the prospect of losing the weight, I was even more excited about the decision. After years—

decades, really—of feeling helpless as I packed on the pounds, I had *done something.* I had *taken control.* I had jumped out of the pot of boiling water.

I knew my listeners would be excited *for* me. But I was still floored by the outpouring of support. Calls and emails and letters. High fives from the doormen in the lobby of our building and atta-boys from strangers in the elevator. And as the pounds kept falling off, guests would come into the studio and do a double take.

It was great to hear things like, "You look *fabulous*!"

It was even better to hear things like, "You look like you're *feeling* good." Because I was! I was sleeping better—no more snoring. I had more energy. I suddenly felt like exploring new things, meeting new people, seizing life by the tail. I could even see my schlong! I look at it all the time now!

But the best thing of all was when someone would confide in me that they, too, were thinking about *doing something* about their weight, or about some other problem that had been plagu-ing them. I'm so grateful to Dr. Oz, and to Dr. Bessler, and to all those nurses—and to Linda and Uncle Johnny and everyone else who supported me before, during, and after the surgery. Alex, most of all. It took a whole lot of people to get me to make that decision, a whole lot of people throwing love and support and encouragement my way. And if I could be one of those people for someone else? What a gift.

My weight-loss journey is far from over. It took me just ten months to lose 120 pounds, but I'll spend the rest of my life working to stay at a healthy weight.

And it *is* work. I work out three or four times a week at one of those fancy gyms full of Oscar-winning actors and other famous faces. I always feel way out of place as my trainer, Charles Cooperman, gets me sweaty. It pays off, though. A couple months into our workouts, I asked Alex if he had changed the seat on our toilet. Alex, of course, had no idea what I was talking about. "It's hard now," I complained. "It used to be more comfortable."

Alex rolled his eyes. "No," he said. "You just finally have a muscle in your butt."

This surgery isn't a magic bullet. And, I should note, there can be complications. I'm a much cheaper date now—where I used to be able to down six martinis, now two drinks will put me flat on my ass.

And as for food, well, our relationship is still hot and heavy. But we've drawn some boundaries. I eat whatever I want, and what I want is almost never a kale salad. But my stomach is smaller than it used to be. So I'll order the mac and cheese, but I'll only be able to eat a quarter of it.

My other relationships are a lot healthier for it. My relationship with Alex. My relationship with my audience. And most of all, my relationship with *myself*.

I started to believe that my life was something worth living to the fullest. I started to stand up straighter, smile wider, wake up excited for the day ahead. Even now, I look at those pictures from my fiftieth birthday, the ones where I'm huge, and I feel a little sad remembering how bad I *felt* back then, but you know? I don't *look* all that bad!

And, um, can we talk about clothes for a second? When I lost my first forty pounds, I had to buy new suits. And that was exciting. Then, a few weeks later, those new suits started to hang off my shrinking frame. So I had to go shopping again. And as my waist got thinner, so did my wallet. I could stroll into Saks Fifth Avenue and buy stuff I *liked* instead of settling for whatever *fit*. I got hooked on buying new clothes.

In fact, I kind of went nuts. My accountant would call me every month to yell at me for spending so much on clothing, which is a much more pleasant conversation than having your doctor yell at you about your blood pressure, but still, it got a little out of control. At one point, I was spending more than thirty thousand dollars a month on clothes. Yes, you read that right. But it was easy to justify. I was starting to do more TV and more appearances onstage at concerts and other events for the radio station. I needed new clothes that fit! Hello! Let's go shopping!

At my lowest I weighed in at about 139 pounds. Friends and listeners told me I was *too* thin. I know I shouldn't admit it, but it was a little thrilling to hear that. Still, they were right. I'd lost so much weight, the extra skin was starting to hang off me. So I decided to do something about that, too, and went in for a face-lift.

That's right, a face-lift. I'm not ashamed. I loved it. I walked out of there looking great and feeling great, and no one should ever apologize for that.

Now that my stomach is expanding (as they said it would), I'm gaining a little weight. My face looks less skeletal. And some of those clothes I bought when I got below 140 are starting to feel too tight. Just the other day, I put on a suit and realized it had gotten too snug to button. Must be time to go shopping!

* * *

Like a lot of people, I spent years and years and years thinking about losing weight—to look better, to feel better, to live longer. I wish I'd taken action sooner.

And I wish that, even back before I was ready to take action, I hadn't beat myself up so much. It does the frog no good to sit there and get mad at himself because he hasn't jumped yet.

For me, the difference was the support I got from others. And when we talk about this stuff on the show, I always make sure to be supportive. If you aren't ready to make a big change in your life, that's just fine—we love you the way you are. If you've tried and failed, that's just fine, too—you're still awesome, and you'll get it next time. The way you look DOES NOT DEFINE YOU. Read that again for me. The way you look DOES NOT DEFINE YOU.

But I love hearing from people who are ready to make that big decision, ready to take that scary step forward—ready to jump out of the pot once and for all. The journey to a better life is long and difficult, but take it from someone who's walked that road: The trip is *totally* worth it.

Unsafe Space

Here's the story of one of the hardest years I've had since I started the show.

It starts in Nashville, Tennessee. I was there to visit St. Jude Children's Research Hospital, which is a legendary facility that does incredible work fighting pediatric cancer. If I wanted to know more about the fight against kids' cancer, I *had* to see what they were doing at St. Jude. Plus, I was just kind of excited to see the place. Danny Thomas, the entertainer, had started it back in the 1960s, and if you grew up watching TV, you knew all about it from the telethons that always featured the era's top stars.

Anyway, when I arrived, I was greeted by my guide for the day, my friend Eric Trump.

Now, this was before his dad ran for president. Not that I didn't know who Donald Trump was. Most people knew him as a rich guy with wacky hair who fired people on a reality TV show.

But to me, and I think to most New Yorkers, Donald Trump was just another in a long line of "only in New York" figures. A caricature of sorts. You'd see him in the pages of the *New York Post*, or showing up in his limo to cut the ribbon at some skyscraper, or holding court in a tuxedo at a fancy dinner. He was almost part of the scenery, kind of like the Naked Cowboy in Times Square. Live in New York long enough, and you'd have an "I saw Donald Trump!" story of your very own.

We'd had him on the show a couple of times. He'd call in, I assume from his office at Trump Tower, and he was always "the Donald"—as in confident. A genius at self-promotion. We mostly just talked about *The Apprentice*. All harmless and fun.

I did know the kids, a little bit. I'd met Ivanka and Don Jr. at different events around town. We'd only talked for a few minutes, but they were perfectly engaging, and they mentioned that they grew up listening to me in New York, which I always like hearing.

But when Steven Levine introduced me to Eric and his lovely then-fiancée, Lara, we *really* hit it off. Like a lot of successful people, Eric had a foundation, and it had committed something like twenty million dollars to St. Jude. But unlike a lot of rich people, Eric actually had a deep passion for the work, not just the headlines he got by sponsoring it.

It was his suggestion that I come down and see St. Jude in person. And that day in Nashville, he gave me the most informative, brilliant tour. He seemed to know everything about the facility and the research being done there. He showed me the lab where they'd come up with a cure for this rare cancer that attacked children's eyes, and the laser beam that allowed doctors to target cancer cells deep within the body without hurting the cells closer to the skin. He was soft-spoken, but his eyes lit up when he dug into the details. I'd always thought he and Lara were sweet, but now I realized that they were passionate and well educated about this most important institution.

At the end of the tour, I thanked them, and they invited me to emcee a fundraiser for St. Jude they were hosting at one of his father's golf clubs. I agreed in a heartbeat. It wound up being another great night. I got to meet some of the kids who were patients at St. Jude, and their parents, and the doctors who were treating them. There were a lot of smiles. And we raised a lot of money.

The next idea we hatched was a walkathon. We came up with a great slogan: "Elvis Trumps Cancer," and decided the route would cross over the Brooklyn Bridge and back and that all the money would go straight to St. Jude to fund the next breakthrough. Who could have a problem with that? Nobody! Even as Donald started to spend more and more time on Twitter voicing his political opinions, I never got any pushback about the charity work I was doing with his son.

I think it was the second or third year we were doing the fundraiser when, as we were walking back toward Manhattan across the bridge, Eric brought up his father's potential run for the presidency.

"Do you think my father has a chance?" Eric asked me.

Truth was, I hadn't thought about it at all. I had heard Donald talking about it, of course, but I didn't think he was serious. I figured it was exactly the sort of thing a TV personality who loved attention would do to push people's buttons and get in the press.

I didn't know if he was a Democrat or a Republican (he's been both). Who cared? I never pictured the Donald in politics.

I just shrugged and said, "Hey, Eric, crazier things have happened."

I grew up in Texas, and—surprise, surprise!—my parents were staunch Republicans.

By the way, why do we only use the word *staunch* in front of the word *Republican*? Can you be a "staunch" Democrat? A "staunch" Katy Perry fan? A "staunch" vegetarian? It's one of those words that, if you say it a few times, starts to sound like it isn't a word at all. Staunch. *Staunch.*

Okay, I'm stalling. I don't *want* to talk about politics! Obviously there are issues we all care about. It's important to be involved in your community. You should always stand up for whatever you believe in. But you have to admit, these days it's a fucking *downer.* I'd much rather talk about anything else, on air and off.

But okay, here goes. My parents were Republicans. *Staunch* ones. They voted for the guy with the *R* next to his name, until someone showed up on the ballot who wasn't a guy at all. Ann Richards. She was tough, and profane, and funny. My mom loved her, even though she was a Democrat running for governor of Texas. My dad? *Hated* her. It was the first time I'd ever heard actual political debate. And mostly they just gave each other good-natured shit, and then went and canceled out each other's vote, and life went on.

What about me? The first time I ever really thought about politics was during the AIDS crisis in the 1980s. Which *shouldn't* have been political, but became that way because of the way the Reagan administration handled it. Over time, I found myself agreeing with Democrats on some issues and Republicans on others.

And when it came time to vote, more often than not, I voted for a person, not a party. I've always looked at candidates and tried to imagine them as leaders. I've worked for leaders who are strong, thoughtful, connected—and I've worked for leaders who aren't. Leadership is a skill, and I know that because I do not have that skill. Which is why I will never run for office. Well, that and everything I told you about my times in Houston.

Anyway, I care a lot about the character of the people who lead us. That's why, like a lot of people, I really liked Barack Obama, even if I didn't agree with him about everything. He seemed so calm, cool, collected. Very presidential. And I *loved* his family.

But some people didn't like him. And you know what? That's okay!

It drives me nuts when a listener (or friend) decides to completely cut you out of their life if you don't agree on the same candidate. It says more about your character than it does about who you're supporting. What it tells me is that you're incapable of having a mature conversation about the facts without losing your shit.

When I'm deciding whether I like you, I don't want to know about your politics.

I want to know that you have an open heart to those you don't always agree with.

I want to know that you're in touch with your truth and not blaming others for your failures.

I want to know that you're not reckless with people's hearts and lives.

I want to know that you'll be cool with me when I'm not cool.

That's the stuff that matters. And yes, politics matters, too. But politics is supposed to be like dental hygiene. You think about it a *lot* occasionally—you brush *really* well the day of your checkup—and then you mostly forget about it until the next appointment. You don't spend all day arguing with strangers online about it. You *definitely* don't break up with friends because they don't floss.

Look, I'm a gay man who hosts a radio show in New York City. I'm pretty outspoken about gay rights, and I think teachers are underpaid, and I surround myself with strong women who aren't afraid to speak up for equality. If you want to call us a bunch of liberal snowflakes, go ahead. But we have people who work on the show who are very conservative in their politics. And we have lots of callers who believe stuff we don't. Sometimes people will call in and say they think homosexuality is wrong. I don't agree with that! But as long as they say it in a way that isn't degrading or ignorant, I'll have a conversation with them.

I don't want to make it sound like I don't have strong opinions. I do. But I have friends and coworkers who have equally strong but completely different opinions. And yet somehow we manage to disagree without going at each other's throats all the time. I know where so-and-so stands on such-and-such issue. She knows where I stand. And if we ever find ourselves talking about it, we're not trying to win an argument. Neither one of us walks away having converted the other. We just walk away with a better understanding of each other's perspective.

I mean, I guess it wouldn't be *politics* if there weren't disagreements. But I just don't understand why you would let those disagreements infect a relationship that means something to you, be it personal or professional. And I *refuse* to let them infect my relationship with my listeners.

Our show—and I know even *this* term has turned into something political—is supposed to be a safe space from politics. You're supposed to be able to say what you think, and we can disagree entirely, and even have a debate about it, but then we all shake hands and move on to talking about Ariana Grande.

Politics isn't what we're here for. And, most important, politics isn't supposed to determine *who* we're here for. Because we're here for *everybody*.

One day, not long after Donald had announced he was running for president, Eric Trump came into the studio to talk about the latest charity work going on in support of St. Jude. This time, he brought along one of those MAKE AMERICA GREAT AGAIN hats you were starting to see popping up everywhere. For some reason, the one he gave me was black. I guess they hadn't settled on red yet. Anyway, I'm not a big hat guy, but I appreciated the gesture, and I put it on for a picture.

Dun-dun-dunnnnnn . . .

I obviously didn't know how serious Donald was about his run for POTUS. But when that picture hit social media, I found out just how serious people were about *him*. There were people yelling at me for wearing the hat, calling me a racist for associating with a known Trump. There were people yelling at Eric, calling him every name in the book. And then there were the people who *supported* Trump. They were just as loud, and a lot of them were more interested in taunting the people who were upset by the picture than they were in promoting their candidate.

Even *then*, I didn't really understand what was happening. I thought Donald's campaign was another Trump publicity stunt, and I thought that everyone who was getting whipped up about it—either for or against—was falling for it.

It wasn't until I watched one of the Republican debates that I started to realize why his campaign had generated such strong emotions. You have to remember, I thought of him primarily as an outspoken, charismatic tycoon who liked partying with models and bragging about his kids. But the Donald Trump I saw on that debate stage was something else. *This guy*, I thought, *is out for blood*. It seemed like he was willing to say or do anything to win.

He sure didn't talk like a typical politician. And that's what got everyone's attention. Everyone else on that stage was clumsy and meek. And, for that matter, there weren't any shiny stars on the other side of the aisle. Hillary Clinton was the only one making noise, and even then, I wasn't totally sold. Like a lot of people, I looked at all the candidates who were running in both parties that year and felt discouraged and disappointed. Every one of them had a good point to make every once in a while. But that's it? We're supposed to vote for the one we're sort of okay with? For PRESIDENT?

We didn't talk about any of this on the show, by the way. Why would we? I'm sure some of us had a candidate we liked, and others of us didn't know who we were going to vote for, but nobody thought it was worth spending time on, let alone arguing about. Let's have a show that can be an oasis from the political hurricane.

Then, in September 2016, we had Eric on the show again to talk about that year's Elvis Trumps Cancer walk for St. Jude. And . . . *holy shit.*

By then, I'd watched enough of Trump on the campaign trail to know that he wasn't the candidate for me (not that I was excited about voting for Hillary, either). But I didn't see why that meant I couldn't talk to Eric about raising money to fight pediatric cancer. He was still as passionate about St. Jude and the kids.

It was one of the most divisive segments we've ever done. We usually keep the text message screen turned off when we have guests in the studio so they don't see a nasty text come across, but on social media, the firestorm was just beginning.

There were a lot of comments like: *You had Eric Trump on?! You must hate women!* On the other hand, there were people screaming at me for not coming out and endorsing Trump. *You must be a Hillary fan—fuck you!*

But the worst part wasn't what people were saying to *me.* It was what they were saying to *each other.* The comments section on our Facebook post about Eric's segment—*a segment about raising money to fight kids' cancer!*—turned into a battle royal. And when we just went ahead and took the post down, people started complaining that we were hiding our support for Trump. Or chickening out because we were supporting Hillary. Then they started arguing with each other about which kind of wrong we were.

My first true taste of "I hate everything about you because of one thing about you." It makes no sense to me!

It was horrible. For one thing, I hate being accused of being something I'm not. But more important, this wasn't the show we wanted to be doing.

Thing is, some radio shows, they can get away with taking a side. There are hosts in our building who decided they wanted to go all in on the Trump movement. There are others who decided they needed to push their audience to take action *against* Trump. Fine. Let them. That's not the lane we want to drive in.

I saw so many good shows tear apart the relationship between host and listener, throwing away a great formula and ignoring what made them successful because they couldn't help but make the show about politics.

My job isn't to divide the world up into us and them. It's to build a place where everyone is welcome.

Well, some people said, *by* not *taking a stand, isn't* that *in and of itself taking a stand?*

Screw that! There are twenty-four hours in a day. You can spend the other twenty taking a stand, and for that matter so can I. But you aren't taking a stand when you brush your teeth, and you aren't taking a stand when you take a poop, and you shouldn't have to take a stand when you listen to the radio on your way into work. And what's more, if you *want* to spend your morning listening to politics talk, you've got lots of options!

I couldn't see any way of covering the election without turning the show into a bitter mess. So we made a new rule. No more politics. Period. We're going to just wait this out.

And when my political friends in New York—on both sides—would beg and plead with me to use the show to get out the vote, reminding me about my responsibility to my country, I heard them. I reminded listeners to vote. But not *for whom*. I felt like

I had a greater responsibility to the listeners—not just to play it down the middle, but not to play the game *at all*.

Not that the listeners were any happier. People would call up and ask, "Why won't you take a side?" And then get mad when I wouldn't take the bait. I hated that. You're not mad at me for not taking a side. You're mad at me for not taking *your* side!

I couldn't *wait* for Election Day to come so this would all be over. That morning, I walked out of the studio, ready to go vote. But then I looked at my phone. Big mistake. The back-and-forth on social media was out of control. People were beating the shit out of me, and our show, and each other. *If you don't vote for Hillary, you're a monster! If you don't vote for Trump, you're a shithead!*

I don't think I've ever been madder at my audience. Or at democracy. I felt like my head was going to explode. I put my phone back in my pocket, turned around, and instead of heading to the polls, I just went home and turned off my phone.

That's right. I didn't vote in 2016. Fuck it. I was fed up with the whole thing.

That night, Alex and I went to bed early, assuming (like everybody else) that Hillary would win. So we missed out on all the excitement (or agony) when the big surprise came around nine thirty and it started to look like Trump had won instead. We didn't find out until we woke up the next morning.

We were both shocked. I knew I had to go to work alongside a lot of people who were going to be devastated. After all, my own politics aside, I work with a lot of young people who live in Manhattan, especially women. Not a super-conservative bunch.

Sure enough, when I got in, several of our staff were crying. And everyone seemed to be in a zombielike state, wandering around the office looking like they hadn't slept in years. People were saying that they were afraid of what our country was going to become.

And I don't know if it was the right thing to say or not—I told you, I hate managing—but I sat everyone down and tried to ease their minds. "Look," I said, "we've got three branches of government. We have checks and balances. Things will self-regulate."

On the air, I told our listeners, "We've had good presidents and bad presidents, and we're still here." Maybe that was a dumb thing to say. I know one thing: We've had good shows and bad shows. And that was one of the worst.

For weeks and weeks, the battle raged on. I told you a few chapters back about the time we had Andy Cohen on the show and it wasn't as fabulous as it should have been. Well, we decided to have him back not long after the election, and this time he came in fired up. Except what he was fired up about was politics. All he wanted to talk about was how awful Trump was, and how his presidency was going to be a disaster.

I didn't know what to do. I didn't want to have another bad interview with a guy I really liked. So I at least tried to engage him, trying to play devil's advocate. I probably actually agreed with a lot of what he was saying, but I wanted to give him something to react to so we could have an actual conversation instead of just a rant. But that backfired, too. Half the audience was pissed at him for going after Trump, and the other half was pissed at me for refusing to go along. (I bet that, reading this paragraph, half of you are pissed that I put up any kind of fight against Andy's attacks on Trump, and the other half of you are pissed that I said I didn't believe in what I was saying. I can't win!)

I'd always thought of elections as opportunities to put our differences behind us once and for all. But this time people retreated even farther into their corners. It felt like the whole country had come down with some horrible sickness that made us glare at each other. Tribalism.

And as much as I wanted to avoid getting into the reasons people were feeling so on edge, I couldn't ignore the fact that this was in the air. When a bunch of people from the show told me they wanted to go down to the Women's March in Washington over inauguration weekend in January, I encouraged them to do it, and to report back so we could talk about it on the air.

Trump-supporting listeners gave us a lot of crap for that. But it wasn't a political statement. If Hillary had won, and there'd been a big MAGA march on Washington, and if people on the show had wanted to go, I would have encouraged them to do it—and I would have asked them to come back to the show and tell us what they saw.

But these days, it feels like saying anything about politics—or saying anything that someone could *interpret* as a statement about politics—is enough to lose you friends forever. We're all on edge, all the time, ready to "cancel" anyone who takes one wrong step.

Aren't we capable of more than that? You may not like it, but I'm capable of taking issue with stuff that Donald Trump says and does and—at the same time!—admiring his son Eric for the work he's done with kids' cancer research.

And you know what? *You're* capable of that, too. That's how we all used to live. We all used to have friends we disagreed with about important stuff but loved for other reasons. We all used to be able to forgive each other for our transgressions. And when those transgressions aren't political, we still can. We all have friends who have let us down—got drunk and said something mean, forgot to water our plants while we were out of town, hooked up with an ex. We don't let the stuff that bothers us about the people we love define them.

So why should we let politics get between us? After all, politics is supposed to be something you *do*. You go to a march. You hold a fundraiser for a candidate you like. You vote on Election Day.

But I think politics has now become something you *are*. It's your *identity*.

And that's a problem. Because it means two people who disagree about some political question can no longer have a conversation about it—or about *anything*. We see each other, and say, *Hey, he's on the other team*, and the dialogue just shuts down.

I've told you that I want our show to be a place where women always win. And we've rejected some of the misogynist jokes a lot of other shows use to get laughs. But over the last couple years, as more women have spoken up about their experiences in our society, I've looked back at the past three decades and seen lots of stuff that today makes me cringe—not just bits we did on the radio, but the crazy shit we did off the air while the songs played.

How about the comfortably nude Greg T? He never had a problem just whipping off every stitch of clothing on command.

We were always entertained by it. How about Butt Bucks, where Greg would pick cash up off the floor with his bare ass cheeks and the listener on the phone won it all! We all knew that, within the confines of our "family," that kind of off-color nonsense is going to happen. But if someone hadn't been comfortable with it, should I have known? Would they have been willing to tell me? Would it have been my fault if they weren't?

I work in the entertainment business, and we're all trying to reckon with the fact that things we used to take for granted won't fly anymore. You'd get fired pretty fast if you got a FedEx package full of cocaine at the studio these days. Used to be, you'd go to a radio convention and there would be strippers at every party, people having sex in the bathroom, total debauchery everywhere.

We replay Phone Taps sometimes, and not long ago we reran one from a decade or so earlier where I played the manager of a hotel. The gag was, I was calling a gay couple who had arranged to have their wedding at the hotel, but I didn't know when we signed the contract that they were two men. "Is there any way we could do a cake without the two guys on top? Could we skip the kiss at the end of the ceremony?"

The joke was on my character—what a jerk he was, and how stupid he sounded. But when we replayed it, we got some calls complaining. *You're a gay man*, some people said. *How could you joke about that?* And you know what? I see their point. I didn't back when we originally did the bit. I do now.

Honestly, between the awful foreign accents and the gay jokes and the gender stereotypes, a lot of our old Phone Taps are no good for replaying anymore. It's a different time. And we're a different show.

But it's hard to function in a world where everything is declared to be either "okay" or "problematic." I don't mind getting feedback from people who think we've gone over the line—in fact, I count on it. And I listen to it. But while "I think that joke was in bad taste" helps me get better as a host, "Fuck you, woman-hater!" doesn't.

We run into the same problem when we talk about cops. Our show has always been pro-police (along with pro-firefighter, pro-military, pro-teacher—anyone who sacrifices to serve the public). It's never been a political thing.

But when Ferguson happened, I realized I had to be careful. We were on the air in St. Louis at the time, and I knew how raw emotions were when it came to the police.

I have no problem acknowledging that there are some bad cops out there. But I still want to speak up and praise the incredible men and women who keep us safe every day. For a long time after Ferguson, every time we'd do a story highlighting some act of police heroism, we'd get nasty comments accusing us of ignoring the victims of police abuse.

Again, I'm not complaining that listeners didn't like something on the show. But when you're in a situation where both sides have something valid to say, the knee-jerk reactions make it impossible for either side to say it.

Look, I'm no political guru. I don't know how to fix our system. But I do know a lot about conversations. I have them for a living. And I try to lead by example on the show.

We disagree with each other *all the time*. We *look* for stuff to argue about. But there's an unspoken agreement that there's something connecting us that's more important than whatever it is we're arguing about. And so, no matter how sharply we disagree, we don't come out of it exhausted and angry. We come out of it feeling uplifted, and like we've learned something about each other. How about we ALL try that out? Can you imagine?

It doesn't cost you anything to be kind to people you don't agree with. And it doesn't get you anywhere to scream at them. Making people feel like shit is not an effective tool for getting them on your side. If you want to try to change someone's mind, don't do it by tearing down what they believe—do it by giving them something new to think about. And be open to seeing it from the other direction—when someone tries to change *your* mind, don't see it as an attack on your identity, but rather as a chance to think about the world from a new perspective.

I know that our political environment is still pretty hot. But maybe you can try thinking about the rest of the world this way: Sit down with someone who isn't like you—someone from a different background, someone with different beliefs, someone who lives a different kind of life—and try having a conversation where you treat those differences as something to be interested in, not something to argue about.

If we're going to get back to a healthier place in our country, I think it has to start with us, not with our leaders. I think we've got to relearn how to talk to each other, and how to give each other space. And yes, sometimes you have to fight for what you believe in. But that doesn't have to be *all* you do. Your political beliefs don't have to define you. And you don't have to let them define anyone else. There's *got* to be something more interesting about all of us.

It's hard, resisting the temptation to get sucked into the back-and-forth, the division, the anger. But I'm gonna keep trying. And if you want to do the same—at least for four hours out of your day—I promise I'll always have a show where you're welcome.

CHAPTER 17

The Gift

Alex and I get very into superstitions. Me, I never walk under ladders, and I'll take a new path if a black cat has crossed mine. But Alex goes the other way. He was born on a Friday the thirteenth, and he refuses to believe his birthday is bad luck. In fact, we always look forward to when the thirteenth happens to fall on a Friday. It did last July, so we had a big party with all our friends. And when everyone had had a couple of drinks, Alex and I got up to thank everyone for coming.

That's when he pulled out an umbrella.

It wasn't raining or anything. In fact, we were inside. And, as you know, opening an umbrella inside is supposed to be bad luck. *What the hell, Alex?* But, as Alex explained, just like he doesn't believe in the superstition about Friday the thirteenth, he doesn't believe in the one about umbrellas, either.

And then, in one motion, he opened the umbrella and dropped

to a knee. And there it was, painted in white on the black umbrella:

ELVIS WILL YOU MARRY ME

The thing you have to understand is that I didn't grow up thinking I'd ever get married—because I didn't grow up believing that two men *could* ever get legally married. It was one of those things that made me different from my straight friends. I wrote it off long ago.

So when Alex and I got engaged, I felt like I was walking into a party that everyone else in the world had been at for hours—and I had no idea how to act.

For example: When you get engaged, the first thing everybody asks is if they can see the ring. I knew that would happen. I've seen movies. What I *didn't* know, until Danielle helpfully explained it to me, was that you're not supposed to take the ring *off* and hand it to people. You're just supposed to display your hand daintily so people can ooh and ahh.

In the video—it's on Instagram—you can tell that I'm really, truly surprised. But apparently I shouldn't have been. We'd had these rings in our apartment for a while, hidden from our view until one of us garnered the courage to ask the other to get married. And I always figured that I would be the only one with that courage . . . one day. So while packing for our month in Santa Fe, I slipped them into my luggage . . . just in case. An hour later, Alex stormed into the living room and demanded to know what I'd done with the rings. "They're missing!"

Dumbass that I am, I couldn't figure out why he was so worried. What, did he think I'd thrown them out? Everybody at work rolled their eyes when I told them that story.

See, I wasn't prepared to be anyone's fiancé. Let alone husband. What a gross word. *Husband*. I liked *boyfriend*. It felt scandalous and sexy. *Partner* was okay, although it kind of sounded like Alex and I had a law firm together, not a relationship. But *husband* is an old people's word.

Then there are all the clichés. Like the one about how Alex was "finally making an honest man out of me." What the hell does *that* mean? We looked it up on the air. Apparently, the idea is that, back in the olden days, premarital sex was *scandalous*, so when you got married, you could stop pretending that you were a virgin. Please, Mary. I've been honest since high school.

And, fuck me, the wedding planning. Immediately, everybody wanted to know if they were going to be invited (Greg T even demanded that he get to officiate the ceremony). How the hell was I supposed to figure this all out? I hadn't spent my whole life planning my dream wedding.

I wasn't ready for any of it. The wedding, the new title, the outpouring of congratulations. None of it. Getting married had never been on my agenda. But everyone suddenly acted like it was going to be the most important moment of my entire life.

Maybe it's the wedding, or maybe it's writing a book about my life, but I've spent a lot of time lately trying to put it all in perspective. I've never been one of those people with a bucket list of life goals I'm checking off one by one. I've never even had a five-year plan.

A couple years ago, I got the strangest phone call from Dennis Clark. Apparently, he'd heard from a friend of ours who served on the Hollywood Walk of Fame committee (my most fabulous friend, Ellen), and there was talk about nominating me for a star on the Walk. Would I be interested? An hour later, my phone rings. It's my publicist, Steven Levine. "Have you heard? I'm going to sell my kidney and help make this happen."

The thing is, getting awards makes me nervous. And I don't mean in that fake-humble "aw, shucks" kind of way. I love people telling me I'm great! Who wouldn't? It's an honor and a huge ego boost, and I appreciate every single one.

But *getting* the award usually means putting on a tuxedo and going to a fancy dinner where I have to get up and give a speech and be the focus of attention. No problem, right? I mean, I speak to millions of people every morning. And walking out onstage at Madison Square Garden to talk to twenty thousand screaming fans doesn't faze me at all. But having to write out remarks and get up behind a podium and address a ballroom? Nightmare.

So usually I don't get too excited about awards. But this one was different. This was the Hollywood Walk of Fame! Would I be *interested*? Are you friggin' *kidding* me? I'll write a check, I'll beg and plead, I'll grab a pickax and dig for the stone myself!

See, if you ask me, the best part about Los Angeles isn't the sunshine or the gorgeous people (most of whom are half plastic anyway). It's the history.

Just like in New York, where it seems like something important has happened on every block, the history of Los Angeles isn't buried. It's alive on every street corner. You can have breakfast at the Waldorf or on the roof at the Peninsula alongside the agents and producers responsible for Hollywood's biggest blockbusters while they make plans for the next one. You can stare up at that big HOLLYWOOD sign like so many aspiring actors who came west to get famous. You can get a drink at the Chateau Marmont hotel, where countless celebrities have lived (and more than a few have died).

And then there's the history right under your feet. You walk out of a drugstore or a coffee shop, and the first thing you see on the ground is the name of some wildly accomplished star. And as you walk down the street, you're taking a walk through the history of American culture. There's Boris Karloff! There's Lucille Ball! There's Bob Hope! There's . . . *ELVIS DURAN?!?!*

It's crazy. It makes no sense. But there it is, at 1717 Vine Street, right across the street from the famous Capitol Records Building. Right next to Luther fucking Vandross. If you ever find yourself out there, you can see it for yourself—and do me a favor: Try to scrape off any gum or dog shit you see.

By the way, let's get something straight about the Hollywood Walk of Fame. I'd always heard that you could just buy a star. Anyone with the cash gets to be a permanent fixture in Hollywood. Which kind of diminishes the honor.

But it turns out that's not actually how it works. First, someone has to nominate you. Then the Hollywood Chamber of Commerce has to vote on and approve your nomination.

Then they tell you that someone has to come up with thirty thousand bucks to pay for it. And, I mean, even that I can understand. It's not like the Hollywood Chamber of Commerce gets a budget from the city or anything. How else are they going to pay for all that stone and brass and gold, plus the guy who makes sure your name is spelled right?

Anyway, in March 2017, there I was, standing between Chris Martin from Coldplay and legendary producer L. A. Reid, being honored with the 2,603rd star on the Hollywood Walk of Fame. Not that I was counting.

The next year, I was inducted into the National Association of Broadcasters Hall of Fame. Another *HOLY SHIT* moment. I'd been watching other people achieve that milestone since I was just a kid in Texas, broadcasting live from my bedroom. In fact, just eight years earlier, Ron Chapman himself had stood on the very same stage to receive the very same honor.

You remember Ron Chapman, right? The guy whose voice got me into radio? "Me and You and a Dog Named Boo"? The feather duster?

Anyway. There's one last chapter to the Ron Chapman story. It took place at an NAB conference in Boston not long after I started at Z100 in the early '90s. I saw Ron across the room, and I couldn't help but run up to introduce myself.

"Hey, Mr. Chapman," I gasped. "My name is Elvis Duran—and because of you, I'm in radio."

He glared at me. "Well, what do you do?"

I beamed. "I do afternoons at Z100 in New York City!"

No reaction from Ron. Finally, he sniffed, "Well, I guess you owe me a thank-you, don'tcha?" And with that, he turned and walked away.

I guess I do. Thank you, Ron.

I told that story at the Hall of Fame dinner in Las Vegas. A whole ballroom full of all the people I'd spent decades looking up to and learning from and laughing with. My idols. My friends. My team. Even Uncle Johnny was there, sitting next to Alex and chugging free drinks.

Earlier that day, I'd taken a walk around the convention floor and marveled at all the exhibits—the new microphones, the digital mixers, the futuristic analytics software for slicing and dicing your online audience.

There's no doubt—this business is *changing*. But it's *always* been changing. We used to use literal tape, and we'd edit it with grease pencils and razor blades. Today, everything's on computers. We used to compete via billboards and prank wars. Today, we have focus groups and professional marketers. And it's been a long time since I did the show high like I used to back in Texas.

But we're still fundamentally doing the same thing we always have. As I told the crowd in my speech, "It's not about transmitters. It's not about ad rates. It's about connecting with people."

And that's timeless. Sometimes people ask me about the "future of radio," and they talk about it like you'd talk about the "future of horse-drawn carriages." As in, there *isn't* one. Except in antique museums.

I always laugh. People have been predicting the demise of radio ever since TV came along. But TV didn't kill radio. And neither did cable. And neither did the Internet.

Why? Because you just can't replace the one-on-one connection you get with radio.

If anything, new technology has given us *more* opportunities to strengthen that connection. We used to rely on phone calls for listener feedback. Then we started taking text messages, so we could see everyone's text on a screen instead of taking one phone call at a time. Then came social media—we can put out a tweet in the morning asking for people's stories about embarrassing first dates and get hundreds in seconds. We all do our own Instagram and Twitter accounts, and it helps our audience feel closer to us. I love it.

A little while back, we had Ed Sheeran on the show, and during the interview, he picked up his guitar and began performing "The A Team." Halfway through the song, and without warning, my emotions caught up to me and I began to tear up. And then I cried.

It wasn't the amazing song he had written and was performing. It was Ed's face. Watching him, I suddenly understood exactly how hard he worked to *give* something of himself to his audience. Every song. Every time. I mean, he must have played that song, what, a thousand times? Ten thousand? But even here, even now, in an empty room, playing it for the 10,001st time in a little radio studio, his whole body and soul were just *pushing* the love outward.

It got me thinking about what our show is really *for.* I mean, yeah, we're there to sell Sleep Number mattresses and all that stuff. But if that's all it was, you wouldn't be reading this book, because I would have burned out and quit long ago.

The addictive part—the part that keeps me coming back every day, the part I can't ever quit—is that our show is fundamentally about *giving* something to the audience. A perspective they may not have considered. An idea that could change their lives. Or even just a laugh while they're sitting in traffic.

A few years ago, we got a call from this girl in junior high school. I forget where. But I remember that she had auditioned for a part in her school musical, and she was crushed when she didn't get it. I guess her teacher had been kind of blunt about it, too—told this girl that she just didn't have the chops for musical theater. Imagine being thirteen, and all you want is to perform, and hearing that.

So I asked her what song she'd auditioned with, and then I asked, "Will you sing it for us?" And she did. And she *killed*. It was beautiful.

When she was done, we all clapped and cheered, and then I told her, "Well, you may not have been able to perform for your school, but you just sang for millions of people—and we all loved it."

There was so much in that moment for me. I felt so happy that she'd had a chance to be heard, and so proud that I could do something to help her recognize how much of a gift she had, and so impressed with the courage she'd shown by agreeing to *sing* on *live radio* for *total strangers*.

And at moments like those, I feel so much less alone in the world. We're all so different, and sometimes it's impossible to find ways to identify with each other, but they're always there. We *all* just want to be heard. To sing our song. To have our moment. To share that special gift that nobody else has to offer.

Whenever we have a young artist on the show and we play their song for the first time, I see the same look in their eyes. They hear their own voice coming through the headphones, and they realize that *their song* is playing on the radio, that people are really *listening*, that the spark they've nurtured in their soul is finally catching fire in the real world. It's *magic*, I'm telling you. Every single time.

I get the same vitamin-E shot every time we hit on a topic that really connects with our listeners. We'll be talking about bad bosses or secret fears or relationship disasters, and we'll get texts from people saying things like, "I feel like you're talking to ME right now!" Sometimes they'll call in and say that because they heard us talking about the thing that's been haunting them, *they* feel less alone.

I don't know where else to get the feeling I get when I hear that. And I don't know what I'd do without it.

CHAPTER 18

A Letter to My Younger Self

Dear Younger Me . . .

This letter is the very last chapter I'm writing before this book is going to press.

(Yes. You're going to write a book. *Everyone* should.)

And that's not the only thing I know about your life that you don't know yet. And a lot of what's going to happen to you is going to teach you important lessons, lessons I had to learn the hard way. So pay attention. I'll even start with the good news.

Your early obsession with radio is going to pay off.

Lesson 1: Listen to your heart, no matter how young you are. You start off your life without all the clutter and static that will build up in your head as you get older. Then you start learning about fear, rejection, disappointment, and self-doubt. As I write this, I'm doing my best to UNLEARN all that bullshit. I always want to tell people to believe in that first voice they hear as a kid. If you love daisies as a child, consider becoming a florist. If you love watching your mom cook dinner, how about learning how to cook and becoming a chef? Almost everyone will try to talk you out of pursuing your childhood dreams. Listen to the few who encourage you to follow those dreams.

You're gay. And shy. And don't have a perfect body. And are sometimes too generous.

Lesson 2: Even though you leaned into being comfortable with your truth when you were a kid, don't let the pressures from others try to lead you to a path THEY believe is correct. That's THEIR path, not yours. Be true to yourself. It's not always an easy road, but it will get you to where you want to be.

You're going to party like a dirty rock star.

Lesson 3: Snorting cocaine (and blasting other drugs) will give you the most temporary high that will quickly dissipate and make you feel like shit. You're one of the lucky ones who will not become an addict. Still, it's a fantastic lesson in avoiding things that bring a short-lived feeling of satisfaction with absolutely no payoff in the future.

You are going to end up in one of the most fabulous, high-paying radio job in the world . . . but that won't mean anything, really.

Lesson 4: You see other people driving expensive cars and living in homes worth millions of dollars . . . and you'll assume that's making them all so fucking happy. Well, there's absolutely no connection between bags of cash and bags of happiness. Happiness doesn't even come in bags. You know what comes in bags? Clutter. You're going to acquire all that stuff and one day realize you want to get rid of it. As I am plotting to do as I write this.

You are going to be scared sometimes. But that's okay. You're going to realize that there's a fine line between fear and excitement. When you do, you'll succeed.

Lesson 5: You have to lose a few times before you win. The more you risk and the more you lose, the sweeter the success will taste when you claim your victories. You'll never know how that feels if you play it safe. Put it all out there.

You'll be tested by others on social media (don't ask, it's horrible) and to your face. They will do their best to try to bring you down and make you feel as if you're the cause of all the strife and problems in this world. They're wrong. Period.

Lesson 6: Understand what makes them say these things. They are self-loathing assholes. Bullies. And will do everything within their power to try and move themselves from the cheap seats to the front row. At your expense. Truth is, they're on their own journey and, hopefully, will make it to a place of contentment and happiness. Not your problem. IGNORE THEM. It'll be challenging, but listening to their vile hatred and whiny, ass-hurt whimpering will get you nowhere. Fuck 'em.

You're going to experience tragedy that will scorch you to your core.

Lesson 7: With every devastating act of earth-shattering WTF scenario you experience, try your best to mourn and process, then pull yourself out enough to learn the lessons you're being taught. And help out others who aren't strong enough to help themselves. Rise above it as best as you can.

You are going to fall in love. More than once.

Lesson 8: Don't be afraid of love. But be careful. Life is going to bring you some doozies. You're going to place several people up on that pedestal to be worshipped, and they're going to disappoint you. And you're going to stay with them, for way too long. Know when to unlock the handcuffs and run like hell. When something is clearly never going to work, realize that you can't fix them. But you can save yourself. And, when you're ready, give someone new your heart to break. You gotta take chances! (See Lesson 5.)

You are going to meet a guy named Dr. Oz.

Lesson 9: Listen to him. He's going to save your life.

You are a good person, and you are going to be okay.

Lesson 10: Finally. Listen to your heart. Listen to your gut. Trust yourself. Be aware of the signs around you telling you what to do and you'll be led to greatness. Allow the Universe to put you in your place. And, at the same time, never forget that you deserve whatever you want out of this life. It's yours.

Love yourself. Be your best friend.

I love you,

Me (older and grayer, but also really fucking happy)

Acknowledgments

Why write a book? Why not just keep the stories inside? What I've learned is that telling your stories, even if only to yourself, makes the journey real. You watch your life being built, brick by brick. You begin to understand how you've ended up sitting where you are as you read this.

The most difficult story to tell is told in silence. Walk into your bathroom. Lock the door. As your face enters the frame of the mirror above the sink, look yourself in the eye. Both eyes. That's you! Have you ever really met this person you're seeing? The person staring back at you is your creation. Is this your best friend you're looking at? If not, make it the rest of your life's goal to make that happen.

Thank you, Mom and Dad, for being my foundation. For a guy who claims to have zero regrets in life, I wish I knew you this well while you were still alive.

Apologies to my brothers, sisters, nieces, and nephews for

making you uneasy with some of these stories. Be thankful you only heard these!

And my newest mom, Barbara. Thank you for helping pick up the pieces every time Alex stormed home all pissed off at me. There'll be more of those, I'm sure. Thank you for letting me marry your son.

Santa Fe. Where it's always warm even on the coldest of days. Always bright and colorful even on the darkest of nights. My little brown town. And my second parents, Drew and Jane, who showed me the way to Santa Fe. I love you.

I don't believe in "relationships that never should have happened." My "big three" ended in heartache, guilt, and frustration, but we learned from them. And for that I'm grateful. And for the others that actually broke my heart, fuck you. And thank you.

Dana, my sister . . . so many years of love. Even though our pillow fights are intense, I thank you for your heart. And for Max. The true love of my life.

Do you have someone in your life who caught you when you were falling? Yeah, me too. If I had to choose friends to lift me up while playing "Light as a Feather," it would be Steve Kingston and Patty Steele, Dennis Clark, Tom Poleman, John Fulham, Linder, Jennifer Leimgruber, Thea Mitchem, Zena Burns, Jeff Smith, Mehmet Oz, Rosanna Scotto, Darren Pfeffer, and Billy Mann. There are more, believe me.

Dee and Scott, who continue to keep the bills paid, the savings account growing, and ME OUT OF PRISON, thank you for always watching over me.

Steven Levine. Go read your chapter again. There's a "thank you" hidden between each paragraph.

Uncle Johny (real spelling with one "n"). Thank you for the

love and laughs. The cocktails and the joints. With or without your toupee, you are always the most handsome man in the room. But, please . . . keep the teeth in.

Dmitriy, who, years ago, merely drove me from place to place. Now he's my brother. And he still drives me from place to place. And argues about the best route to take. He's always right. Oh, the stories Dmitriy could tell about everything he's seen in the backseat of that Escalade.

Susy, always Max's favorite aunt and angel. And Susie, who keeps the Santa Fe light on for us. Pat Peck, another sister, who beautifully made our houses into homes . . . and always knows to the penny how much is in my checking account. Then spends it.

How lucky have I been to meet and interview the artists who give life to the notes and lyrics on the page. And, some of them appreciate that I introduced you to them. Most of them are in and out of my life only while they promote their latest releases. Only a few of them are in my phone contacts. I'm more like you. A fan. Not a close friend. I'm happy with that.

And to the hardworking men and women who back up the music. The managers and music company leaders . . . some I've known for almost forty years! Thank you for the music.

A shout-out to the radio geeks. Who, like me, grew up with a desire to be a star but were too awkward to walk across a stage. As I always say: We aren't celebrities. We are toothbrushes. People use us every day. They depend on us to be there when they need us. They would miss us if we left them. So, we show up.

Actually, our voices are more than just sound. A voice is an idea. An opinion. Encouragement. Praise. Warmth. A voice is a friend.

"We are in the friendship business," said Bob Pittman. The

ultimate radio geek. Thanks to you and Rich Bressler for your years of support and for opening your mind to where I believe it should all go next.

Andy Barr wrote this book. I just talked his ear off. Andy, you'll never know how much I appreciate you and how you've taken mixed-up moments and turned them into stories. Thank you for your patience. God knows you need a lot of it with me. Wanna write another one? I DARE YOU.

The first real-life publishing professional who gave me a chance, Mitch Hoffman. You so beautifully mask your bulldog strength with a most encouraging, gentle voice. How lucky am I to have you represent me for this first book? And Matthew Benjamin at Atria. The first time I walked into your offices at Simon & Schuster, I felt so insignificant and out of place. Seriously, y'all. This is the house that published Ernest Hemingway, Jackie Collins, Stephen King, Howard Stern, Harold Robbins, F. Scott Fitzgerald . . . and Elvis Duran? Matthew, thank you. After meeting you and your colleagues, I now know publishing people are as freaky as radio people.

To my partner (not the boyfriend kind) David Katz. Thank you for holding my hand every step of the way. You always prove that I'm worth more than I give myself credit for. You ask for the ridiculous and get it. Look at what we've accomplished. Look at where we can still go! You've rightfully earned your "agent's percentage" of everything you negotiated. More important, you've snagged 100 percent of my gratitude and appreciation. What a deal!

The morning radio family you and I love. Without them I would stay in bed and hide under the sheets. They make me laugh, cry, think, feel. They make me smarter and wiser. They sometimes piss me off. I piss them off even more. There are butterflies in my stomach as I look at these names. Each one of them is on their own journey and deserve the stars. They ARE the stars in my life.

I think we met in this order: Danielle, Skeery, Greg T, Scotty, Brody, Garrett, Froggy, Coaster Boy Josh, Producer Sam, Web Girl Kathleen, Nate, Jake, Gandhi, and Diamond. And my kids that left the nest and continue to succeed in radio . . . the teams of TJ & Loren and Carla Marie & Anthony. Christine Nagy, Carolina Bermudez, and Bald Freak Ronnie. We even have past interns who are becoming superstars out there. I'm a proud papa.

Hang on. Almost done. Saved the best for last.

To you. You've had me at my best and worst. You heard laughter and encouragement when, a few times, I was covering up sadness and fright. You see, on those many cold, dark days throughout these decades behind the mic, I've easily suspended the monsters for four hours. Between 6:00 a.m. and 10:00 a.m. it's you and me. You have been the place I go to forget about whatever it is that scares me. I may not know you by name, but I know you have a story. You deserve happiness. And smiles. And puppies. And sunny beaches. And laughs. Lots of laughs. And love. Thank you for being there.

And Alex. Every single time we should have ended it, we didn't. We ignored all the others and fought to make it work because down deep we always knew this was meant to be. We're both stubborn, loud, and emotional. The three traits people tend to run from are the ones that keep us together. Our thing is far from textbook perfect. And, I'm learning, that works best for us. Thank you for being the most meaningful gift I've ever opened. As I said pages before this: *No matter where I am and whatever I'm doing in this world, I would always rather be alone with you.*

And Max.

About the Author

ELVIS DURAN is one of America's most well-known and widely admired media personalities. His nationally syndicated radio program, *Elvis Duran and the Morning Show*, is America's most listened-to Top 40 morning show and one of the ten most listened-to programs in all of radio, heard live by nearly ten million people in more than eighty markets across the country. Meanwhile, Elvis's regular appearances on NBC's *Today, Late Night with Jimmy Fallon, Entertainment Tonight,* and other television shows have made him not just a beloved voice but a familiar face for fans of pop culture.